UNDERSTANDING YOUR PARTNER'S LOVE LANGUAGE

12 SECRETS ON HOW BETTER COMMUNICATION WILL HELP YOU BUILD A HEALTHY AND HAPPY RELATIONSHIP

RACHEL BURGESS

Rachel Burgess

By reading this document, the reader agrees that under no circumstances is the author responsible for any losses, direct or indirect, which are incurred as a result of the use of information contained within this document, including, but not limited to, — errors, omissions, or inaccuracies.

"I'm not telling you it is going to be easy- I am telling you it is going to be worth it."

Art Williams

CONTENTS

Do you find it challenging conversing with your spouse? Are you tired of debating and fighting with your husband or wife whenever you engage in conversation? Is your partner no longer talking to you?

Relationship communication issues start because each one of us is a flawed person. We may have certain differences in hairstyle, preferences, attitudes, etc., but nobody has the same things that we do. So, when we communicate with one another, it's not unusual to observe that we can have difficulties. Every one of us sees things differently, has different and opposing views. It is by knowing the people around you, the people in your relationship, that you can learn to accept that we are different beings.

Communication in relationships is a frequent issue for men and women regardless of background. Married couples usually have a lot of interaction communication and relationship issues because the people involved in the relationship don't want to listen. Many guys want ladies to pay attention to them, particularly when they converse about marital issues. They really want the woman to make the changes. Place a dot at the end of their sentence, that's IT!

This episode could have been the worst headache of any woman. Conversing without really responding, for the most part, to a man's side, is very infuriating and annoying. This is especially true if you haven't settled the argument yet and he does not want to talk anymore. Relationship communication problems emerged from the unwillingness of men to settle relationship problems.

Many couples (including us) have had to deal with these communication issues at some stage in their marriage, and it's not fun! Screaming, yelling, anger, frustration, resentment-it can definitely be unbearable and could even kill your willingness not only to effectively communicate with your husband or wife, but also to savor your relationship. But you don't have to unnecessarily worry about that

Effective communication is no exception to a happy marriage. It's natural to bicker and even have minor fights with your partner because you both have your own ideas and your own thoughts. But if things get out of the way, it can damage the marriage.

Irrespective of whatever communication problems you're struggling with, you can learn how to communicate effectively with your spouse today.

Whether you feel that you're not being heard, that you can't hear your spouse, or that you want to communicate better with your spouse without fighting or screaming, this book will show you how.

Get everything you could ever need from relationship books to couples in one convenient title equals to understanding your partner's love language. This workbook contains a number of immersive activities and structured interactions that will help you solidify your communication skills, strengthen your connection and resolve potential issues.

Whether you're working out specific issues in your relationship or just looking to bond as a couple, this standout among relationship books for couples—covering everything from finances to sex—provides you with an all-encompassing exploration of your romantic partnership, this book is an excellent 'How-To Guide' for practicing the key skills that will help you identify and overcome communication barriers and achieve relationship success with the important people in your life--your spouse or partner, child or children, parents, siblings, friends, co-workers, customers--everyone!

As a former school teacher and a relationship expert, At forty-one, now a wife and a mother of three, I have mastered the art of nurturing and exhorting not just young ones but humans in general, with extreme patience, kindness, and empathy.

As a relationship and parenting coach who has taught monthly parenting classes, hosted and spoken at different parenting and relationship workshops, written helpful, instructional books. Thus, I have decided to come up with this relationship communication guide to teach readers to communicate with less blame and more

Understanding your partner's love language teaches readers how to connect effectively and get more out of marriage. If you're talking to your boss, trying to persuade your mom, or romancing your significant other, the value of effective communication in your day-to-day life is inevitable. Through the strategies outlined in this essential guide, you can become a better communicator, practice open communication, and be able to handle almost any situation with self-belief and compassion. Every person is wired differently for love, with different habits, needs, and reactions to conflict.

The great news is that so many people's thinking work in similar ways and react well to security, attachment, and rituals, making it possible for the brain to be neurologically more loving and less conflict-ridden.

This workbook is a guide to understanding the mind of your partner and able to enjoy a loving relationship established on respect and commitment. Analyzing research findings on how and why love lasts from psychology, family systems, and emotional control, this book presents twelve core principles that can enhance any relationship.

Married life or some other kind of loving relationship between a male and a female is a fantastic thing, and no couple should permit the threat of poor communication to bring an undeserved end to such a delightful union. Arguments, struggles, and misunderstandings among couples can go a long way to destroying a long-term marriage in split seconds. It can also be compared to cancer in the sense that if it is not treated with any sense of urgency, it could eat deeply after a long stay in the relationship and could cause irredeemable damage to your marital life.

It's vital that you don't allow this marital and relationship threat to put your relationship through unnecessary anguish when you have a solution.

So keep your eyes glued and let me walk you through the journey towards making your communication in your relationship and marriage a beautiful one.

KNOW YOUR COMMUNICATION STYLES

Have you at any point talked to a companion, relative, or your partner and felt, ideally, just for the moment that you could not communicate? Somehow, regardless of how you attempted to account for yourself, the other individual didn't seem to understand and didn't "get it."

Communication between two people can be essential, pure, and streaming or it very well may be difficult, stressed, and choked. So much relies on communication style.

I recollect an experiment in which two people were set in front of an audience to talk. The first two speakers appeared to indeed battle and couldn't prop a progression of conversation up. For this situation, the communication problem had to do with speed.

One of the speakers had a fast style of talking, terminating words, expressions, and sentences rapidly and absent many deferrals. The other speaker had a usually moderate pace, rambling forward a couple of words, wavering, thinking, and afterward communicating a couple of more words. The fast speaker continued talking, not allowing the slower speaker to ring in.

The next two speakers were usually exceptionally moderate. One talked, both paused, quietness for quite a while. The subsequent individual talked. Both paused. Another time of quietness, that conversation flowed, but at an agonizingly slow pace, making it difficult for the relentless people in the crowd to remain associated and tune in.

And afterwards, the last two speakers started to talk. Each spoke quicker than the other, hopping into the conversation, interfering with the other, and shooting out their words without breaking a sweat. These were two usually quick speakers.

Even though that experiment was interesting to me at that point, from that point forward, I have discovered that there are many different styles of talking and communicating. Whether the pace is quick or moderate is only one of many elaborate differences between two speakers.

Each individual has an exceptional communication style, a manner by which they collaborate and trade data with others.

Thus, this takes us to have a more profound glance at the four basic communication styles that people use to convey in relationships which are: passive, aggressive, passive-aggressive, and assertive.

It's critical to understand every communication style and why people use them. For instance, the assertive communication style has been seen as best since it fuses the best parts of the various styles.

When we separate these four styles, we'll better understand each style's attributes, standard expressions, and what makes them one of a kind.

The first communication style is known as the passive style. People who utilize the passive communication style regularly act indifferently, respecting others. For the most part, passive communicators neglect to communicate their sentiments or requirements, permitting others to communicate. Much of the time, a passive communicator's absence of outward communication can prompt misunderstanding, outrage, or resentment. But passive communicators are also simple to coexist as they tailor others and "accept the way things are."

Instances of expressions that the people who

utilize a passive communication style would state or may accept include:

"It truly doesn't make a difference that much."

"I simply need to keep harmony."

The aggressive style which is the second style is regularly evident when somebody conveys aggressively. You'll hear it, see it and even feel it.

The aggressive communication style is accentuated by talking in a loud and demanding voice, keeping in touch and ruling or controlling others by accusing, scaring, reprimanding, compromising, or assaulting them, among different qualities.

Instances of expressions that an aggressive communicator would utilize include:

"I'm correct, and you're off-base."

"I'll get my direction regardless."

"It's all your shortcomings.

Passive-aggressive communication style clients seem passive on a superficial level, but inside the person may feel weak or stuck, developing a resentment that prompts fuming or carrying on in inconspicuous, indirect, or mysterious ways.

Passive-aggressive communicators may likewise seem agreeable, but may quietly be doing the inverse.

At last, passive-aggressive communicators know

about their needs, but now and again battle to voice them.

Instances of expressions that a passive-aggressive communicator would utilize include:

"That is fine with me, but don't be astonished if another person gets frantic."

"Indeed, we can do things your way" (at that point mumbles to self that "your way" is moronic).

Thought-to-be the best type of communication, the assertive communication style includes an open communication connection while not domineering. Assertive communicators can communicate their own needs, wants, thoughts, and sentiments while also thinking about others' requirements. Assertive communicators focus on the two sides to win in a circumstance, offsetting their privileges with the privileges of others.

One of the keys to assertive communication is utilizing "I" statements, for example, "I feel disappointed when you are late for a gathering," or, "I don't care for clarifying this again and again." It demonstrates responsibility for and practices without accusing the other individual.

Instances of expressions an assertive communicator would utilize include:

"We are similarly qualified to communicate consciously with each other."

"I understand I have options in my life, and I think about my choices."

"I regard the privileges of others."

To become an Assertive communicator, understanding how others impart can be vital to conveying the desired information to them. So as to build up a more assertive communication style, here are a couple of tips to remember: Take possession (use "I" statements), keep in touch, figure out how to state "no", and always voice your requirements and wants unquestionably.

COMMUNICATION STYLES IN RELATIONSHIPS AMONG COUPLES AND SPOUSES

Most couples do have different communication styles. Sexual orientation, age, childhood, instruction, social differences, personality type, past relationship history, and many different elements come into play when it comes to how we communicate.

But did you realize that you and your partner can communicate differently and still have a stable, happy relationship?

Reliable communication doesn't necessitate that you share information or handle conflict the very same way. Indeed, it's regularly our differences that make us all the more intriguing and appealing to someone else.

The ideal approach to improving your relationship is by studying your partner's communication style, just as your own. Here are four kinds of communication styles you may perceive.

Amplifier and Condenser Communication Style is a typical communication difference is the style of the "amplifier" and the "condenser."

These terms were instituted by creator and therapist Dr. Norman Wright, who says an amplifier is "somebody who communicates by sharing what they need to state in incredible volumes of subtleties."

A condenser is one "who is most happy with sharing minimal more than what is completely vital."

As an amplifier, you may feel baffled that your condenser spouse doesn't talk more about musings and sentiments and doesn't share enough detail. You may learn about being disengaged or cut.

A condenser may feel overpowered and overflowed with the entirety of the data the amplifier shares. An excessive number of words feel diverting and pointless.

The solution: Amplifiers can work on truncating their musings and clarifications when they verbalize them to their condenser partner.

They can work out their musings and concentrate the key focuses on verbalizing or talking it out with another amplifier before speaking with their condenser partner.

Condensers can put forth a more considerable amount of an attempt to verbalize contemplations and emotions with the amplifier partner, realizing that sharing more will make association and closeness.

Another communication style difference is competitive versus dependent. If you have a more dependent style, you need to unite people to work out problems.

When a choice should be made, you're probably going to carry your partner into the effective procedure and ask their supposition before you choose.

A competitive communicator is more arranged toward force, rivalry, and strength in their communication style. In general, their conversations will be more assertive, and testing and they want to settle on choices all alone without much or any contribution from others.

The solution: Dependent communicators can

feel injured when their partner doesn't offer a similar agreeable communication process.

They should solicit their competitive partners ahead of time from a conversation to share and examine an issue in a more agreeable manner.

The competitive partner will do well to temper them regularly, want to go only at transparently challenge their partner. They can figure out how to tune in and welcome criticism before communicating their musings, regardless of whether it feels like an exercise in futility.

As regards direct and Indirect communication Style, there are two essential ways spouses communicate what they need: either directly or indirectly.

One of you may be direct, and when you need, want, or feel something, you have no problem coming right out and saying it.

However, one of you may be more indirect and will keep down on precisely what you need, need, or feel.

You may state it in a more indirect, unclear way. For instance, this partner may state, "I'm thinking about whether there's an occupation out there that may pay you more."

When these two different communicators are in

a relationship, there's a more noteworthy open door for strain and stress.

The solution: Direct communicators need to recollect that their words can be twisted or insult their partner.

The more indirect partner needs to figure out precisely what they mean without shrinking away from the real issue.

This may feel awkward for somebody who cares to hold nothing back, with training, you can figure out how to express your real thoughts without being cruel or coldhearted.

Another style is the hot and Cold Communication Style. During struggle or genuine conversations, there are regularly two different ways you will move toward the circumstance. The partner who utilizes a "hot style" needs to immediately connect to put the issue out there and complete it.

If the problem isn't settled quickly, this partner feels restless, troubled, or engrossed.

The partner with the "cold style" doesn't do well with this exceptional and quick methodology. The individual in question needs an ideal opportunity to thoroughly consider things, but not seemingly out of the blue.

The solution: The hot style communicator feels

the immense strain on diminishing the pressure, but the individual can figure out how to step back, take a full breath, and give the other partner time to process their feelings.

The cold style communicator needs to regard how much uneasiness it makes for their hot style partner to defer imparting. It can aggravate things much if you deliberately hold out excessively long.

THE LANGUAGE OF LOVE

We are altogether unique and experience the world in one of a kind ways. We have to ensure we are conveying such that the beneficiary understands it, and the equivalent is genuine when it comes to love. Is it true that you are exhibiting your love for your partner such that they will hear and understand it?

In general, we will give love in the manner in which we want to receive it - which may not be a similar path as our partner. So the entirety of your endeavors might be futile, and they might be feeling rather unloved.

The Love Language system can be precious in helping us understand ourselves and our partners better. But what makes the use of this knowledge conceivable is merciful and legitimate communication with your partner, coupled with a certifiable want to share joy and association."

Read ahead to get a once-over on the five primary love languages, just as some useful bits of knowledge on how you and your significant other can identify them in one another and, all the more critically, influence them in your relationship

The first is the act of service, with demonstrations of service, it's everything about the need to feel like your partner esteems you and is eager to invest an unmistakable exertion in showing their appreciation.

If your Love Language is "Demonstrations of Service," you feel generally loved and acknowledged when your partner contemplates what they can do to facilitate the obligations that are burdening you. Hearing "let me help you with that" or "I previously dealt with it" is more energizing to you than those photos of hot folks with infant creatures (indeed, it is a whole book). Apathy, inability to play out a lot of errands, or being oblivious with how they can help you are all simple ways for you to feel undervalued and unloved.

With respect to words of affirmation, If you ache for compliments from your partner or calling you pet names make you blush, this may be your love language. Much the same as touch, this sort of talk has a range, so ensure you and your partner understand where your specific range lies, clarifies Dr. Chuba. Does hearing how appealing turn you on? Or then again, do you appreciate a more express sort of language?"

If your partner longs for words of attestation, leave a careful note in their vehicle or send sweet messages on more than one occasion per day. Remember, when unique events move around, it's everything about the words you put in the card.

The quality time love language is a love language that more people need to get settled with because the more significant part of us is so surged and separated in our day by day that we have overlooked how to just 'be' together.

For you, nothing says "I love you" like marathon watching Game of Thrones or playing Scrabble on a Friday night. Having your partner's full focus is the time when you feel generally valued. Interruptions during quality time or deferring dates can cause you to feel like you aren't critical to your partner. Booking the time to be together is urgent to the achievement of your relationship.

Accepting gifts as a love language may seem as though it's materialistic or saved for gold diggers. But if this is your language, don't scrutinize your character. It has more to do with the idea behind the gift than the gift itself. You welcome the mindfulness behind gift-giving (regardless of whether it's a marvelous birthday present or bringing home your preferred magazine from an excursion to the drugstore). All gifts, regardless of whether little and every day or vast and incredible, remind you how much you matter to your partner and how much care and exertion they believe you're worth. Missed birthday events or negligent gifts are your relationships bad dream since it causes you to feel like your partner couldn't care less about you.

First of all: Physical touch doesn't generally compare to being sexual. "Physical touch sounds basic enough when applied to sex, but many people don't understand that touch is a language and communicates expectation.

"Most importantly, it's significant for an individual with this love language to understand their own needs and limits around touch, and afterward communicate them to their partner. For this, it assists with considering touch a range: On the one side, you have dispassionate touch, and on the contrary, you have sexual touch, with changing kinds and degrees of touch in the middle."

For example, a terrible day may require an embrace, a night out on the town out, clasping hands; and on your film night in, you can exploit some nestling.

So why is knowing your partner's love language so critical to the accomplishment of your relationship?

WHY YOU NEED TO KNOW YOUR PARTNER'S LOVE LANGUAGE

It will enable you and your partner to feel more valued - consider it: if you're a "Demonstrations of Service" individual dating a "Words of Affirmation" individual, your partner may shower you with compliments and "I love you"s consistently, but you would spend the relationship not feeling genuinely refreshing in light of the fact that they never offer to get things done or do the dishes. Understanding your partner's love language will assist you with observing how they show their love, so you do feel loved and acknowledged, knowing the manner by which they give their love is different than yours.

Another major reason is that It will permit you to communicate your needs more. We've all had those easily overlooked details we wish our partner would simply manage without us asking; complimenting us when we spruce up, bringing home blossoms, arranging a night out on the town. When they don't do these things, it very well may be destructive on the grounds that in our brains, those things compare to their appreciation. We likewise may stress they'd simply be doing those things since they feel compelled to if we ask them to, not out of thankfulness or love.

It will show you and your partner what you both ought to manage without being inquired.

Knowing your partner as a "Physical Touch" individual will make you more insightful about holding their hand in broad daylight or embracing them when they're down, and you will have the option to understand the significance and significance behind these little demonstrations that, for you, would somehow be insignificant. Your partner will be more cognizant about what they can do to show you how much they acknowledge and love you. When you and your partner both know how different gives thankfulness and wants to receive gratefulness, it puts forth for more nice choices and attempts that cause you and your partner both to feel loved and esteemed.

All in all, how would you decide your other half's

love language? One path is to consider how they show their love for you. "Look at how your partner communicates his/her love language.

What and how we express love and want is regularly what we need to respond to. collaborations with companions, family, and even associates can reveal pieces of information, calling attention to "how you and your partner's families express love can likewise offer knowledge on your love languages.

In a perfect world, the entirety of the 5 love languages ought to be a piece of your relationship. However, there's consistently one that needs to be given first concern.

Put forth an attempt to understand what your partner needs so as to feel loved and satisfied. It might be contrary to what your love language is, and that is OK. This isn't an opposition. Or maybe, it's unrestricted love.

DISCOVER YOUR PARTNER'S NEEDS

We all need to be seen, heard, and understood. We particularly need this from our partners. We need our partners to say, Yes, I am tuning in. Indeed, I get it. Honestly, I understand your pain. I'm sorry it hurts you, and I am here. We need our partners to be keen on and think about what's going on inside our souls.

Wanting to be seen and heard and understood are fundamental human needs.

Do you love bread as much as some do? Do you know what your needs and wants are in a relationship? Think about your relationship needs like being your bread, and your wants resemble jam. Contingent upon what your love style is, you're going to need and need different things to satisfy you.

HOW MEN'S NEEDS DIFFER FROM WOMEN'S NEEDS

Both men and women stroll into a relationship looking for very similar things: the Love, the support, and the glow. However, amusingly, each thinks that it's difficult to convey those needs to the next! Expecting obviously that the two players are mentally steady, they happen to love one another and need that relationship to go on until the end of time.

As it happens that both genders have similar essential characters and know their partners need them too. It just leaves space for pondering; why are we battling? How about we see?

As regards love and affection. Men want a woman whom they can spoil; pour all their Love and consideration over. A woman can fulfill each female job he'd ever need in his life, whether the closest companion, a lover, an associate or even a mother. So, in all honesty, men are romantic, they love flame light suppers and that feeling where they carry joy to another person. Consider it a self-agreeable system, but men aren't excessively narrow-minded all things considered!

Women need to feel loved and uncommon, to

feel that somebody loves everything about her, and above all, continually convey the message that she's needed. In this manner, if her primary need is disregarded or if the message doesn't get past, that would cause a significant strain in the relationship that may never recuperate!

Men think Women Want to feel loved also. Still, most men live by this code "If you aren't requesting more, at that point I'm carrying out my responsibility right" since men know women to be this annoyingly demanding animals that if a small segment of their need is missing they'd transform men's lives into a horrific experience, till it's only how they need it to be!!

Women think men need to be loved more than they need to offer Love; that they think that it's more pleasant down at the less than desirable finish of the rope to the degree of demanding the sort of affection where if they're gone women simply quit living till they choose to mount over their overinflated ego and come back to spare lives!!

Concerning communication, Men need fair based communications, where a woman would address questions with no concealed messages, for they would prefer not to guess what anybody might be thinking or go through days attempting to understand signals when it could pause for a moment if just their partners would be clear about it. The main concern is that men lean toward straight forward conversations as long as the woman's sufficiently keen to know when and how.

Women need their words to be heard, a man who is a decent audience resembles a rare jewel. Since the more significant part of the time they needn't bother with a solution, they possibly need to express their real thoughts. When they need one, they'll request it; at precisely that point, one may begin appealing to God for men to locate a proper solution, rather than "everything will be OK"!

Men think women need them to take care of whatever problem they're griping about. By enlightening them concerning their sentiments, certain things are normal, among which men should cause the wellspring of disturbance to disappear.

Women think men need them to be shallow, stay silent when it goes to their needs and wants, and ideally manage them all alone because they'll be deserted! Furthermore, because women accept that men need no conversation whatsoever, they use manipulation, believing it's the best way to be heard without pushing her man away

When it comes to commitment and fidelity, men

need commitment as much as women; it's merely a question of affirmation. Men set aside longer effort to ensure that they picked the correct woman and presumably had more opportunity to get over their commitment issues! Other than that, they need a similar strength, the home, and a safe place. Moreover, when it comes to infidelity, it's a significant issue to men precisely as it's to women, without any exemptions or reasons.

Each woman wants the commitment, the security, knowing that she has a man - limited whom she can love and love. Men know women need commitment, such a given that even though women likewise experience cold feet, it's considerably less dangerous. In reality, most women can hardly wait to submit, they're known as commitment monstrosities!

But it's where men think women like to focus on a player is the place they're off-base, for women who need relationships never need players. Without a doubt, they'd feel unique if a player picked them over every single other woman, but rather than that little voice inside notice that a man may be cheating, they'll be left with loud alarm's shouts driving them to craziness!

Women think men endure commitment hypersensitivities that they'd just submit on physical levels, and whenever they locate a more alluring "female," they'd drool all over her and leave! It went to a typical conviction that men can't be trusted to be reliable; they'd run whenever things get only somewhat extreme, and they don't appear to deal with the entire relationship pushing ahead requirements that well!

Regarding support, Men need to achieve things with no help whatesoever from others. Sure they'd need women to inquire as to whether they need it to which they'll for the most part answer with a no but ideally to end at that as opposed to being compelled to receive the help they never needed in any case. Women need to have the support they need without requesting it honestly; women deserve such treatment in relationships! Men think women need NO SUPPORT, having confidence in the truism "treat people how you need to be dealt with" in this manner out of not having any desire to sound excessively pushy, as long as women don't request it, men won't volunteer to do it!

One thing you need to know is that the more women love, the more they offer support; in this way, support is an indication of Love. That is why women will, in general, feel disillusioned when men don't offer that. Women think men need extraordinary support! That is, that's all anyone needs to know, just rapidly move to the following point.

HOW TO UNDERSTAND WHAT YOUR PARTNER NEEDS

The majority of us have a perceptual predisposition in the manner we communicate. Is your partner a more significant amount of a hearable individual who likes to talk and tune in? Or then again, would they say they are more open to visual information, inclining toward loads of eye to eye connection or seeing your words put vigorously? Maybe your partner inclines toward sensation communication or the boost of touch and needs real consolation on the head of verbal communication.

If you know their perceptual predisposition, you can change your communication style to work with theirs and eventually discover how to get enthusiasm back in your relationship. By being delicate to one another's inclinations, you will get a higher amount of the excitement and affection you need.

When you're on the same wavelength as your partner, you can work to all the more likely understand how to address each other's issues. These manifest from multiple points of view as there are people, but they all return to six fundamental human needs.

The essential human need is a certainty, and it should be agreeable, appreciate the joy, and maintain a strategic distance from the pain. An individual with manly vitality can meet the certainty needed by being sincerely present, transparent for their female vitality partners, in any event, when they are disturbed. Somebody with ladylike vitality can address this issue by showing their manly vitality partners that their love is unqualified – saying as much, but being available and abstaining from pulling back in any event, when things turn out badly. Next to zero enthusiasm in a relationship is frequently the consequence of uncertainty – but not the valuable sort of uncertainty.

Variety is the subsequent human need since we can practice and exhibit our physical and passionate range just when difficulties and variety are available. Every relationship has manly and ladylike vitality.. Manly empowered partners can address this issue by starting surprise dates or token gifts with their lady-like partners. Female partners can address this issue by being more provocative, and by, for those hoping to zest up the room, amazing indeed. Absence of energy in a relationship can sometimes be the consequence of straightforward fatigue, so infusing a little uncertainty into romantic experiences can stir up the everyday practice and reignite enthusiasm.

The third is to feel significance, required, uncommon, and needed. Anybody can address this issue by considering different ways they can show their partner how significant they are. What little thing would you be able to do today, this week or this month to show your partner that there is nobody else on Earth who could have their spot? What would you be able to do to show how appreciative you are for their love? How would you be able to show them their uniqueness is valued? When you center around being your partner's main fan, getting energy back in your relationship turns out to be more straightforward.

Fourth is love and connection with others. You can best address this issue for your partner by understanding how they experience the world and how they like to receive love. If your partner is exceptionally visual, they will love it if you look at them or wear their preferred garments; if your partner loves acts of kindness, even a little gift will mean everything to them.

The fifth human need is growth, because, without enthusiastic, scholarly, and otherworldly development, we can't ascend to our latent capacity. This is valid for people, but it's similarly as valid for relationships. If you're not developing, you're kicking the bucket. Put in the work that it takes to understand one another and find creative approaches to make things work for both of you to address the absence of energy in your relationship.

The sixth and last need is contribution and giving. Giving is the key to riches and fulfillment. What might you do to make the individual you love upbeat? Okay, anticipate something consequently, or is seeing them in a beautiful state enough? When we give without desire and spotlight on gratefulness, we give energy a spot to thrive.

From these six fundamental human needs, you can start to figure out your partner's fundamental beliefs. Viably, what is critical to your partner?

When identified, you can start to interface with your partner on that level. But, how would you make sense of their guiding principle in any case? Tune in.

Listening is most likely more required than you may understand. It's more than just trusting that your turn will talk, for instance. Or maybe, listening includes a lot of perception also. To put forth a conscious attempt to understand your partner's needs, it's essential to know them.

Watch your partner. Observe things to which they react—physical touch, getting to know each other, having a conversation, gifts, and so forth.

Tuning in to your partner is critical to associate with them. Without tuning in, it's about difficult to know them, not to mention interface with them genuinely.

Indeed, even in the happiest relationships, there will be disagreements and strife. It's prevalent and typical and can be reliable if taken care of, such that it tends to your needs and your partner's needs. Time and again, when there is a struggle, you need to win. You need to be correct. You need your own needs met, and you don't consider meeting the other person's. Regardless of whether you "win" the battle, you're only setting yourself up for another. Perceiving and figuring out how to address your partner's issues isn't just a decent method to treat the individual you love. It's likewise a decent method to carry satisfaction to your relationship and, like this, to you.

HERE ARE FIVE WAYS YOU CAN USE TO MEET PARTNER'S MOST FUNDAMENTAL NEEDS:

The first is respect, if your relationship were a house, respect would be the foundation the house sits on. Without it, a relationship can't be sincerely sound. Limits are as often as possible crossed when there isn't respect among partners, and not acknowledging an individual's limits causes dependable resentment and outrage. One approach to show that you respect your partner is by showing sympathy. By consistently tuning in to their considerations and emotions, and validating them, you'll help fabricate closeness and respect for their independence.

Time and attention is the second one. Great relationships don't occur unintentionally. For most of us, accomplishing a happy, stable relationship includes learning many new abilities and placing in a great deal of difficult work. Perhaps the ideal approach to satisfy your partner is by giving the person in question time and attention. By concentrating on your partner while they are talking or while you're partaking in a movement together, you will cause them to feel significant, supported, seen, and acknowledged for their identity.

Affection is typically a piece of enthusiastic foreplay and sex, but necessary affection should likewise have a spot in your relationship. Embracing, kissing, and clasping hands are mostly instances of natural ways you can show affection for your partner. Saying "I love you" and offering words of thanks and caring are verbal showcases of affection that are significant, as well.

Another major need is approval, as a youngster, you looked for approval from your folks and overseers. Regardless of whether your folks met this longing, you keep on needing approval and support from your loved ones and whose supposition you esteem. It doesn't require a ton of exertion to show your partner you support, and essential compliments are a decent spot to begin.

Security, certainty, and consistency is another way to meet your partner's needs. Life will toss many difficulties at you and change is unavoidable, regardless of whether it's a new position or the passing of a parent or another life-modifying occasion. Your relationship with your partner should offer you both a protected base while you travel through life. Consistency and consistency offer this sort of security. You need your partner to be there for you and be solid consistently, so you should be dependable to them, as well.

SIGNS YOU MAY NOT BE FULFILLING YOUR PARTNER'S EMOTIONAL NEEDS

When you're in a relationship, it can get normal to fall into specific propensities. Making suspicions, however, that these examples are usually the most beneficial, can be perilous. It's imperative to check-in and ensure that you satisfy your partner's needs emotionally, so your relationship can remain as stable as workable as long as possible.If you are not accommodating your partner's emotional needs, your partner will probably be sad and unfulfilled. While you don't have to feel exclusively liable for your partner's prosperity, you ought to have the option to examine and give a decent measure of emotional solace.

On the other side, neglected emotional needs will, in general, yield up even in the subtlest manners.

Here are hidden signs you may not be satisfying your partner's emotional needs, as indicated by specialists.

One is that You Fight All the Time. While a

partner whose emotional needs are neglected may ice you out, they may likewise raise your regular arguments into out and out fights, not knowing what else to do with their repressed feelings.

"If you and your partner appear to have similar arguments repeatedly, it could be an indication that you do not completely understand the hidden emotional need every one of you is attempting to meet," Williamson says. A partner who feels misunderstood may get sufficiently baffled to fight more than if they were feeling secure in their relationship.

Another sign is when your partner is more physically distant. Physical closeness isn't about merely sex. Also, a partner who feels an absence of emotional closeness may begin drawing endlessly from physical closeness.

Physical distance can incorporate little things, such as non-sexual touch (handholding, snuggling, embracing), When emotional needs go neglected, there is commonly a physical pullback, whether it be obvious or little." Checking into whether this separation has been a little change or becoming over an all-inclusive timeframe can help you make sense of if this is a significant issue.

One other major pointer is that your partner has to beg for validation. You may not see what your partner is cautioning you of just underneath the surface if you've made the suspicion that your relationship is excellent. But a partner who is prone to request that you compliment or validate them might be looking for comfort you aren't giving as of now.

"If your partner is continually looking for emotional validation — by requesting that you welcome them, [or] acknowledge something they have done — at that point you may not be giving them the emotional support and validation that they need," David Bennett, certified instructor, and relationship master, tells Bustle. This sort of validation-chasing might be particularly evident if your partner's love language is words of certification.

The significant point here is to consider your partner's needs while communicating yours.

If you don't communicate this, you risk your partner believing that you are entirely mindful that their needs are just a need when it's advantageous for you or some unintended message.

Sometimes, your needs will struggle with each other, and you will need to talk about it, arrange it, and go to a compromise together.

Relationships flourish when needs are met and waver when they're most certainly not. That reality, just, is non-debatable.

Try as much as could be expected to address your partner's issues consistently and know it might be with a touch of uneasiness but get it done!

Presently watch your partner and relish in their bliss, and I guarantee you, beneficial things will be returning to you.

Begin joining this training into your typical daily practice. Before you know it, addressing your partner's needs and how they like them to be met will have provoked an adjustment in you, and it won't be unnatural any longer.

3

GET TO KNOW YOUR PARTNER DAILY

How well do you know your partner? Do they have the characteristics that help you improve as an individual? Do they have habits that make you mull over your relationship? Have you gotten the opportunity to become acquainted with both the best and the most exceedingly awful parts about them?

These are the questions that, if answered, can help you understand if you're with the ideal partner or not. However, you should likewise remember that not all relationships are their best, and keeping a receptive outlook about which defects merit your understanding is significant.

Knowing each other is one of the most significant of all the relationship-building aptitudes accessible to submitted couples. This relationship-building ability is undoubtedly known by couples who have expertly constructed a passionate durable marriage or a passionate severe enduring relationship.

The 'knowledge' you know about your partner recognizes this relationship from every other relationship. Nobody should know you just as your partner. Furthermore, if they do, it is a problem; it implies you and your partner need closeness. Also, for particular couples, this could be an admonition indication of genuine relationship inconvenience.

A passionate marriage or serious relationship is one in which you and your partner have intimate knowledge.

Sexual closeness is a genuine case of what it intends to 'know' one another. It is usual for you to strip for your partner and that person for you. At that point, you energize, animate, and joy each other in manners allowed to nobody else. In doing this, you find out about one another's bodies and personal feelings. This sexual closeness is just a single significant method of 'knowing' one another. Sexual knowledge is reasonable, agreeable, and sound, and when proceeded after some time will fabricate you and your partner a passionate marriage.

HOW WELL DO YOU KNOW YOUR PARTNER?

This is an old question that most people have posed to themselves sooner or later in their lives. Regardless of what we like, your partner has contemplations and feelings that you don't know anything about.

How regularly have you arrived at a spot in your life with somebody you think you know, as well as possible, to find that they keep on astonishing you? The amazement may be lovely about something truly astonishing they have done in their carries on with that you had no clue about.

Or on the other hand, the astonishment may prompt a disappointment in a behavior that you didn't know they were prepared to do.

What does this mean? You can go through an entire lifetime with an individual and not so much know who they are by any stretch of the imagination. Similar to the entire planet we live on, we are continually changing and adjusting to our environment.

Today, you are necessarily a result of your entire life's experiences and your reactions to them. How you think, feel, and carry on as a result of every one of that has transpired before this time.

What's more, how you will be tomorrow will be a

result of everyone that has occurred in the past, notwithstanding what you experience today and the choices you make about yourself as well as other people as an outcome of that experience.

Your partner may have expectations and dreams that are shrouded somewhere inside that you would never envision. Perhaps your partner doesn't feel good imparting these musings to you. Furthermore, perhaps you don't feel good sharing either. This doesn't make you a "terrible" couple. It just methods you resemble the average couple out there.

To begin with, let me get straight to the point. This is not a poor reflection on you. What will be? You can't uncover data from underneath an individual if they prefer not to impart it to you, or can you?

I talked with a lady today named Susan, who met a serviceman a couple of months back. The two have been occupied with their lives, thus had not fraternized before he was requested to go into service. He did not recount his crucial leaving and, in this manner, couldn't let Susan know where he would have been or when he would be back.

Five weeks have now gone with no communication, and Susan is pondering where he is. Has he gone into a combat area where he can't communicate with her? Or more awful despite everything has he gone to some injustice, or is he purposely maintaining a strategic distance from her?

Her disarray about this stems mostly from her not so much knowing him all around ok to know what may be the reality. As I said to her, each couple needs a particular time together to truly become more acquainted with one another toward the start of a relationship in any case frailties will regularly sneak in.

Presently, while I have said that you are continually changing and this ought to expect you to be continually open to finding who your partners are once more, there is likewise an incentive in discovering where your partners have originated from; their initial life experiences just as the experiences of their kin and guardians. This data will help you figure out the guiding principle of this conceivable partner, especially regarding you as a couple.

Concerning communication in relationships, most couples never become more acquainted with one another on the profound, close level that they could. People fear being helpless. They fear dismissal. That is the primary concern.

There is regularly a feeling of, "I won't share if

you won't share as well." This is understandable. What's more, it's human nature.

People must be in a circumstance that feels sheltered and secure before they are eager to open up and disclose advantaged data about themselves. If you need your partner to impart to you, you should make an environment that advances that.

Not very far in the past, society appeared to compel people to air every one of their considerations and feelings to anyone (Oprah, Phil Donahue, Sally Jesse Raphael, and now Dr. Phil). However, that vehicle of telling the world your most profound, haziest insider facts has now been, to a great extent, supplanted by this new thing called the unscripted TV drama.

But what do we see time after time? People air their most profound musings and feelings on TV and are later crucified for their genuineness. That is passed along to others, and that is why you don't share it if you don't need to, but this mystery isn't useful for marriage.

Your partner, and perhaps you, have similar feelings of trepidation. What if I tell this individual all that I have inside and afterward: They snicker at me, they don't understand me, they later leave or separation me and take that data with them

People neglect to acknowledge that if they share everything, it incredibly cuts the chances that the relationship will end.

Communication problems in relationships are one of the most widely recognized reasons for separation and separations. (As I would like to think, practically every different problem originates from the absence of communication in relationships.)

What you need is complete instruments to slug-proof your relationship or marriage using love questions that burrow profoundly and genuinely permit you to know the individual you love. Since the communication goes the two different ways, your partner will turn out to be more open to sharing their inward most musings since you will feel good sharing.

So what may be a portion of the things that may be important for you to find out about your partner?

The questions are unending and could incorporate how they obtained their name, their family ancestry, their preferred things, how their folks settle clashes, how they settle clashes, what their relationship resembled with their kin growing up and what their expectations are for their future.

This takes us to the following part of this guide,

which has to do with the crucial questions to ask your partner.

MOST IMPORTANT QUESTIONS TO GET TO KNOW YOUR PARTNER

A fascinating aspect regarding relationships knows about your partner. Frequently, these are what we are excited about during the dating time frame. We are frequently energized and curious about what folks consider us, and men, too, regularly get some information about what women like.

Without a doubt, it is in dating that we will, in general, ask so many inquiries about one another. However, becoming more acquainted with one another ought not to end in the wake of dating. In marriage as well, you can add more flavor to your relationship through specific questions for couples. Sometimes, wedded couples don't think about asking those senseless 'whys' and 'what if' questions we frequently brought out during dating. Those may sound senseless, but by bringing up issues that way, we will, in general, know more about the convictions and estimations of our partners. It can help us decide how good we are with our partners, and as it were, knowing the odds of making a successful marriage.

These are a couple and fundamental questions to get some information about each classification that should give you a thought about what they know about you and in any event make you talk. The more conversation, the better, so if one question turns off the subject, let it occur, you may find more than you expected!

WHAT IS YOUR FONDEST, UNREALIZED DREAM?

Thinking about your undiscovered dreams can help put you on the way towards what's to come. Other than that it's consistently critical to communicate enthusiasm for your partner's objectives. When you and your partner bond over your objectives for the future, you can have a superior thought of supporting each other to make those dreams a reality.

WHAT'S YOUR MOST EMBARRASSING MOMENT?

If you could have any activity on the planet, what might it be? What heritage do you trust you leave the world with? What was your most humiliating moment? As indicated by Earnshaw, it's critical to ask open-finished inquiries, for example, to show your partner that you're interested in them. Regardless of how long you've been together, there's continually something new to learn. Sharing fun stories from before, or trading thoughts on provocative questions can genuinely help you see different sides of your partner.

HOW DO YOU FEEL ABOUT ...?

Love maps are tied in with knowing your partner on a more profound level. When you've been with them for quite a while, it's difficult to accept that you know each and everything there is to know about them like their preferences or aversions. People are continually developing and evolving." So it's essential to continue posing questions about their attention and feelings. Don't only expect that you know what your partner wants or doesn't need since you feel like you definitely "know" them.

WHO WOULD YOU SAY BE YOUR CLOSEST FRIENDS? WHAT ABOUT ENEMIES?

Who you decide to keep around you can say a ton regarding you. For example, it can show you the sort of characteristics you esteem most in your companionships. It's not just essential to know who your partner's companions are, and it's likewise a smart thought to know about the people who give them inconvenience. Show that you consider their kinships and their new moving relationships by being available to talk about them

WHAT IS THE BIGGEST SOURCE OF STRESS IN YOUR LIFE RIGHT NOW?

Stress is a significant piece of the entirety of our lives, opening up to your partner about the stress in yours and permitting them to vent to you can unite you. You will be unable to tackle each other's problems. But being an attentive person and giving them a compassionate shoulder to incline toward can extend your bond.

WHAT IS YOUR GREATEST FEAR?

Answers to questions about your biggest fear, your present objectives, your preferred café, or your fantasy get-away may change after some time. To stay up with your partner's latest, it's OK to pose similar questions once more. "Answers may change with time as your relationship advances, so make it a highlight. Do numerous love maps after some time to remain current on one another's inward operations and heart musings," Cosgrove says.

Building love maps for your relationship is a continuous thing. It's entirely difficult to state that you know everything there is to know about an individual since people are continually evolving. If you manage to remain curious about your partner, you can continue learning new things for quite a long time.

Other questions to ask are:

- What was the best moment of your life before you met me?
- What was the most exceedingly awful moment of your life before you met me?
- What is the one thing you need to achieve to feel like your life was not squandered?
- What is your preferred activity when I'm nowhere to be found?
- What's one thing about you that would astonish me most if I knew it?
- Who has had the greatest effect on your life and why?

- Who is your legend, and why?
- What is your preferred trademark about me?
- What was the principal thing that attracted you to me?
- What causes you to feel safe?
- What is your biggest fear?
- Why do you love me?

You may be expected to know the appropriate responses, but what if you are incorrect? Loads of people THINK they know everything about their partners, but they are regularly off-base.

SOME CRUCIAL THINGS TO KNOW ABOUT YOUR PARTNER IN A RELATIONSHIP

In many relationships, couples like to think they have each other made sense of following quite a while of being together, however, there still could be a long way to go! You'd be charmingly astonished to discover what your partner does or doesn't know about you.

Here are some key things you should know about your partner if you need to guarantee you know them.

Knowing the life story of your partner – both the great and the terrible parts is quite important. Many people have faith in love from the outset, and they state that it tends to be the beginning of something beautiful. However, many people took in their exercises the most challenging way possible and understood that love isn't sufficient to make a relationship last.

You additionally need different variables, and one significant one is to become more acquainted with your partner for who he/she is – and it doesn't stop there. You additionally need to completely acknowledge what you can find as you disentangle their life story, particularly the awful parts.

Another important thing is their preferred things – and people. Make a rundown of the things and people that can make them grin and discover it in your heart to cherish them. Significantly, you know about these significant bits of your significant other's life. Besides showing that you care, it's an insightful method of acknowledging the truth that her satisfaction can emerge from different sources – not merely from you and your relationship.

You also have to know the memories that make them cry. Understanding pity and how people keep tragic memories can help you become more acquainted with an individual better. By knowing what makes the love of your life cry, by attempting to contact them and make this connection, you are making a shelter that they can generally rush to whenever they feel separated.

Recollect that relationships are not just about romance. Besides being a lover, you are likewise a companion, a dependable associate, and an ever-supportive partner.

Learn to know their dreams and yearnings as well. What are the things that they anticipate? What are the objectives and aspirations that they have chosen to seek? Know your partner better by valuing their courage and their certainty to confront the future without questions.

It's a moving thing to know how your partner sees herself ten to quite a while from now, and it's such a pleasing feeling, that you are with somebody who isn't hesitant to reach skyward and think beyond practical boundaries.

A rundown of the things and habits that bother your partner is one other pertinent thing you should know. Each individual has a rundown of things that bother them. Knowing each thing on your partner's rundown is hugely significant, with the goal that you can make the fundamental adjustments and maintain a strategic distance from the typical frivolous arguments.

However, much as could reasonably be expected, attempt to understand that you are two different people with extraordinary experiences. Making a compromise is one bit nearer to making a more grounded connection, particularly if you're new in the relationship.

In conclusion, in particular, you need to know if you are a part of your partner's vision of things to come. What is your career path five years from now? Do you frequently talk about your life together and how you wish to go through it with them?

Knowing your partner better and finding the things, habits, and occasions that contribute to how they see the world can have any kind of effect and can help your relationship endure the trial of time. Once more, ask the correct questions and don't be reluctant to hear the appropriate responses.

Indisputably, you can without much of a stretch improve your marriage or serious relationship by putting additional time and exertion into getting within scoop about your partner. Simultaneously you have to find better approaches to fix a messed up marriage or a severe relationship that needs excitement and warmth.

When you and your partner have completed this study of marriage or serious relationship questions, trade them, and alternate examining and posing questions about everything. This is a chance to get the opportunity to 'know' each other better and construct a passionate marriage or serious relationship.

Make up your questions.asking each other questions alternatively yourself as an approach to showing your partner more subtleties is imperative. When the person in question answers mistakenly or offers a fragmented response, simply include the significant subtleties.

4

DON'T LIE. BE HONEST AND OPEN

Honesty is, no doubt, a vital piece of living a happy, cultivated, and moral life. The ideas driving honesty are among the main things that kids are taught, and Honesty is empowered in pretty much every scene of life. Thomas Jefferson said "honesty is the primary part in the book of insight." The issue with Honesty is that in crude structure, it is a quest for the truth, and the truth is different for each living individual.

When it comes to being honest with your spouse, it is undoubtedly a significant part of marriage. But there is Honesty at the time and honesty that unleashes from a lifetime of living. The individual inside us all has many insider facts, and verifiably many ought not to be shared even with a spouse. Life discloses to us that even as unpredictably as we know an individual, there does not genuinely know anybody entirely but oneself! Look how many tales about evil grotesqueness that originate from people who carry on with appear to be brimming with Honesty and respect. It appears that Honesty is alright and acknowledged as long as the truth that we tell is too. Being honest and the whole idea of Honesty is a dumbfounding best-case scenario.

To shape a stable relationship with somebody and become emotionally cozy, you have to impart experiences and privileged insights to your partner that you don't impart to any other person. That sort of exceptional, cozy, profoundly private exchange requires the two players to be honest. Honesty includes giving exact data about occasions that are known or have just happened.

Honesty is coming clean as you know it about verifiable occasions that have just happened. Honest partners in a stable relationship don't knowingly give deception. However, being honest doesn't mean being inconsiderate, unpleasant, or forceful. It doesn't mean sharing things to hurt your partner or "holding nothing back." Discretion — utilizing decision making ability about what to uncover and what not to uncover — is significant in any stable relationship.

So it's typically best not to assault your sweetheart's new attire or offer comments about another woman's "hotness." It isn't essential to share these feelings, and doing so may hurt your partner.

Who might argue that it is anything but a smart thought, to be honest? But many husbands and spouses look at dishonesty as a smart thought under specific conditions. The truth of the matter is that marriages are demolished by dishonesty, not by Honesty.

If a spouse doesn't give honest and open communication, trust can be subverted, and feelings of security can be decimated. At that point, you can't confide in the signs that are being sent, and you have no establishments on which to assemble a healthy relationship. Rather than developing together, you become separated. Now let's look at the different degrees of Honesty.

Emotional honesty reveals your emotional responses - both positive and negative - to your life's occasions, especially to your spouse's behavior. You need a consistent progression of exact information from one another. Honesty empowers a couple to make fitting adjustments to one another. Both of you are developing and changing with each new day, and you should continually conform to one another's changes. But if you're not getting exact data, you can't make the best possible adjustments. Honest feelings should be communicated and received. Grumblings must be heard and regarded.

Historical Honesty shows information about your history, especially occasions that show individual shortcomings or disappointment. Whatever humiliating experiences or genuine slip-ups are from quite a while ago, you must tell the truth with that person. The tendencies that drove you to accomplish something in your past are as yet a piece of your temperament, and the impacts of specific circumstances have formed what your identity is. These things should be shared. Likewise, this implies you ought to uncover any past sexual relationships if you are going to understand one another.

Current honesty shows information about the occasions of your day. Give your spouse a schedule of exercises, with an extraordinary accentuation on those that may influence your spouse. In great marriages, couples become so reliant that sharing an everyday plan is necessary to coordinate exercises. When exercises are blameless, it's significant for your partner to understand what you do with your time. Ensure you're anything but difficult to track down in a crisis or when your partner simply wants to make proper acquaintance during the day.

Future honesty exhibits your attention and plans in regards to future exercises and targets. Do nothing without an eager agreement among you and your spouse. If you respect your spouse, you will need information and support from him/her on the choice and agreement on the heading.

With complete honesty, don't leave your spouse with a false impression about your attention, feelings, habits, likes, detests, personal history, day by day exercises, or plans for what's to come. Don't purposely keep individual information from your spouse.

THE COMPLEX TRUTH ABOUT LYING TO YOUR PARTNER

The truth is, we as people always lie. Social researchers acknowledge it as a profoundly human quality. The most famous and socially capable among us are typically the greatest liars of all. The reasons we have for lying are nothing unexpected. They extend from honest to evil: We would prefer not to hurt the people we care about, we need to control the observation others have of us, we need to keep up or raise our status, we lie to secure our narrow-minded interests, and we need to control others. But as fundamental as lying is by all accounts to human creatures, believing relationships are additionally an essential human need, and as we as a whole know, lying annihilates trust.

Research shows that little lies make it simpler to lie. When you include self-justification, sometimes the lies become so enormous you begin to believe them yourself until you are caught and compelled to support the relationship-harming results that break down the bond you have and may, at last, cut off devastating the association.

Lies regularly start as self-protection but, for the most part, go to implosion. It isn't unexpected to feel that the outcomes of coming clean exceed the danger of lying, but in any event, when you don't get captured, a lie frequently harms the relationship.

I once worked with a client who went through more than a year in treatment, talking about his objective to locate an extraordinary partner, and keeping in mind that he had the option to meet a few great women; he continued asking why he was unable to feel near them. While we investigated different elements from his family and past relationships, he appeared to be genuinely sure that the problem was that he had quite recently not yet discovered "the one," and that he should keep looking.

I agreed this was conceivable, but I asked him to explain for what good reason he was so sure of that before we proceeded onward. He expressed to me that the women he was dating must be defective, because all he could do was lie and undermine them, and still they all affirmed to love him. As anyone might expect, he had never mentioned the lying and cheating and was in reality, likewise lying to his advisor. He had practically no understanding of the way that his lies and relationships with different women on the double were keeping him from finding what he truly needed, which was an extraordinary, close bond with one woman. It had never happened to him that these women didn't love him; they loved the individual he was claiming to be, and this was something he feared most.

If I asked him why he lied to them, he said he

would not like to hurt them. If I asked why he precluded from treatment the way he was seeing different people without a moment's delay, he expressed that he would not like to look terrible. He thought the lies he was telling were self-saving when they were extremely self-undermining.

Presently, while it is anything but complicated to name this individual as basically narcissistic, the truth is that the vast majority's lies come from a comparative want to self-protect somehow or another, but are at last foolish, because lying, regardless of whether you don't get captured, keeps you from having something a great many people need, which is a credible connection and bond with another human being.

Does the goal make a difference? People frequently believe that their aims justify the lie. Lying not to offend another person is kinder than harming them, isn't that so? This kind of lying is a dangerous slant. My client above justified his lying to various women by saying that he would not like to hurt them, which in one respect was right; the higher truth, however, was that he needed to control their discernment and would not like to get discovered accomplishing something he knew was terrible enough that he expected to lie about it. His lie wasn't about their feelings; it was about his expectation to manipulate and control. What about the lies of exclusion? What if you never really say something that isn't true? Is that an escape clause that lets you free? Suppose you lie or intentionally forget about relevant data to abstain from harming another person that, at last, is tied in with concealing your behavior. In that case, you can be guaranteed you have gone too far and are abusing the privilege your partner needs to make his/her own decision about whether your behavior is satisfactory or not.

I know life isn't simple, and there are perplexing purposes behind why people deceive. But it merits considering what these lies cost you as far as having a superior, more profound, more close connection. Perhaps not generally, honesty is the best approach, but that well-known adage is unquestionably more regularly directly than wrong.

Consequently, this will lead us to another significant part of being honest in a relationship, which is the idea of being open in a relationship.

KEEPING AN OPEN COMMUNICATION WITH YOUR PARTNER

The success of a relationship depends on how well the couple is alluded to communicates and helps out one another. However, being honest takes a considerable amount of mental courage for many people. Taking everything into account, mentioning to people what you genuinely think and feel places you in a particularly frail state. For specific people, being helpless is the height of losing control. This can make it difficult for you to be open with your partner, whether you are hitched to them. A couple of people are significantly more pondering and spared about their feelings, and this can make it difficult for them to state what they truly think and feel.

In this way, we routinely develop fortifications around our spirits and shield ourselves from trusting in others. This can cause any number of problems in relationships, and a couple of couples are even divided because of an inability to be emotionally open with each other.

Relationships are never straightforward, meaning they take a tremendous amount of work. Still, if you push through all the difficulties and aggravation, you can find ways to emotionally communicate better with your partner. Relationships are connected to making a life with another person. As opposed to family, you choose to have that person in your life since you significantly love and care for them. Both of you have experienced tremendous and awful, and you profoundly regard the respect you have for one another.

Relationships take a vast amount of intricate work to make them work - I don't think I have ever heard of a perfect relationship. If you have, well, that individual is in all probability lying. Everyone has a couple of essential qualifications that they must have in a relationship. For a couple, honesty bests works, while for others, sex is above being wealthy. Notwithstanding the way that these are genuinely basic to have in a relationship, I believe communication, especially open communication, is a huge factor in making a relationship truly work. If you and your partner know how to communicate with each other, by then, you have a stable relationship. It's an exceptional feeling knowing you can go to your partner with any concern or thought and know they are going to respect and identify with you. But being direct with your partner isn't everyone's strong suit. It will take practice and affirmation to get it on target.

It's fundamental to trust in each other to make

your relationship last. Coming up next are some shown techniques for making sense of how to open up emotionally without overcompensating.

HOW TO OPEN UP TO YOUR PARTNER IN YOUR RELATIONSHIP

Know your feelings first, When you know your feelings, it's simpler to identify how you'd feel in a specific circumstance. What are your body's sensations? What are the feelings related to those sensations? What are the circumstances or people who can make your heart hurt and your chest tight? What causes you to feel down?

If you experience difficulty identifying your sensations and feelings, utilize a word reference, or a speedy Google look and record all the words identified with feelings. When you're not mindful of each of those terms, you can't know how you'll feel when you open up emotionally.

One other method towards opening up to your partner is to have an open dialogue. You need to quit utilizing one-worded answers. It's difficult for specific people to be open when all they are getting is a "yes" or a "no" answer in a conversation. While single expressions are immediate, they don't generally clarify a great deal. What's more, that is the general purpose of being more open with your emotions.

You need to account for yourself, be defenseless, and not be hesitant to be open. I generally attempt to disclose this to my beau. I need our relationship to be open with criticism and discourse consistently. Communication is vital in any relationship, but if one individual is doing the majority of the emotional talking, it may very well be an uneven relationship, and that doesn't profit anybody.

Being open and powerless can be a terrifying thing. But it's smarter to do as such than to begin being angry and lament not doing it in any case. With these essential tips, you will be headed to an emotionally steady relationship.

You can also open up by talking about your past pains. While talking about exes isn't recommended in new relationships, there are circumstances when you should talk about your past pains. Not exclusively will you show you confide in your partner, but you'll likewise help them understand your pain, behavior in specific circumstances, and your weakness.

Above all, it's a decent method to open up emotionally. Who knows, possibly you'll feel a liberating sensation once you share your previous pains instead of attempting to work them out yourself.

Abstain from playing a casualty, however. If you haven't recuperated from your past relationship yet, your partner probably won't believe you. Abstain from rebuffing your partner for the mix-ups that your exes made

To maintain an open relationship, be completely honest. There's no reason for opening up emotionally when you're not coming clean. If you doubt your partner's response, it's smarter to hold up until you know. However, if you believe your partner and they support you, guarantee you're 100% honest.

It's dubious, and you may even feel embarrassed from the outset. Grasp it. 100% honesty will make your relationship more grounded and breed trust. When you need to open up emotionally, even a harmless exaggeration can hurt your relationship, so reconsider before telling it.

To be open in your relationship, you have to stop laying blames on your partner. Finally, when you're figuring out how to open up emotionally, you should quit refusing to accept responsibility for the issues at hand. Nobody is liable for you being emotionally inaccessible – neither your folks nor your ex-partner.

They may adversely influence your emotional

wellbeing, but you're the one in particular who can allow them to do as such. Rather than accusing others, face your fears and let them go.

Turning out to be open emotionally with your partner must be your decision too. If you open up because your partner lets you know along these lines, don't fault them. You generally have a decision.

Figuring out how to open up emotionally requires gradual steps, time, and exertion. In particular, it must be your own decision. If you feel pressure, let your partner know about it. Request that they give you time. Try not to open up in light of weight.

The exact opposite thing you need to manage is feeling liable for opening up emotionally with an inappropriate individual. Know who to trust in any case.

Ways not to get your partner to open up

You can get your partner to open up, but first, let's take a gander at what you ought not to do as you may perceive a portion of these behaviors and will need to stop them now.

- Getting angry with your partner and demanding that they mention to you what's going on

- Accusing your partner of keeping insider facts and making presumptions about what those privileged insights might be.
- Shouting and causing arguments just to send them to the brink thinking this will get them to talk.
- Making them feel liable and disliking them. If there is a mystery, they, as of now, feel liable enough without your help.
- Let your partner know that you love them unequivocally. That you know that they might be reluctant to reveal to you whatever it is that is annoying them but that you guarantee to tune in without judging or blowing up.
- Listen to your partner and hear what they need to state. Many people tune in but don't hear. Work on tuning in without interference, don't attempt to fill quiets or holes in the conversation. When you talk an excessive amount of you don't allow the other individual to be heard.
- Do not react protectively to an argument. Consider what has been

stated, if your partner is correct, say as much.

- If your partner begins to open up, let them know you are tuning in and hearing them, avoid including your comments, and finish what they need to state. There are many times when we as a whole simply need to be heard.
- If you have to apologize, I will not joke about this. It tends to be so natural to state grief, just to do something very similar once more. Your partner needs to know that you are heartbroken, not trying to say the words to mollify them.

Knowing how to communicate your feelings is critical to having an emotionally satisfying relationship. Opening up and being defenseless makes closeness. But being able to share your feelings goes past saying, "I love you." Excellent communication likewise implies having the option to communicate when you're feeling emotions that are awkward like bitterness, disappointment, or outrage. Having the option to impart your feelings to your partner doesn't come effectively to everybody. But with some time and a little work, it is possible for anybody.

These are a portion of the means you can take to get your partner to open up. There are many others, but this is the beginning stage. Take these activities, and your partner will feel safe, you will expand on your communication, it's dependent upon you to make a move to save your relationship.

5

ALWAYS BE PRESENT IN YOUR RELATIONSHIP

A significant part of relating to someone else is remaining in the present with them and taking immediate impressions of their activities, words, and feelings, and afterward having the option to react unexpectedly. So regularly, we are urgently worried about what impression we are making on others, we have minimal inner space for taking in any new impression of them.

Accordingly, we become restricted in our view of them. For this situation, we limit our recognition by envisioning them to receive us, and it might have nothing to do with what is going on with them. It is likewise challenging to remain right now with someone else if we now have an all-around shaped previously established inclination of what their identity is—our pre-shaped mental representation channels how we decipher any new impressions of them.

Our minds arrange our experience by bringing the past relationship to a new experience. The goal is to place new data into old classes rapidly and frequently pass up on the chance for another experience. To keep this programmed work from totally commanding how we take in new impressions, we need to put forth a conscious attempt not to do as such. If we can't frame new affiliations, we stall out in tedious experiences and frequently wind up stuck in the usual, worn-out clashes with people.

When you love somebody, the best thing you can offer is your presence. How would you be able to love if you are not there?

You know that feeling you get when you're talking to your partner or spouse, and they don't appear to be "there?" By that, I mean, a piece of them is elsewhere, and it's not with you. You may ponder where their mind is, or feel offended or hurt that they're not entirely present in your organization. Sometimes our mind meanders, which is normal, and it can happen when we're with somebody we care about who's talking to us. Still, if we are completely present when we're with the individual we love, our spotlight and attention are on them, particularly when they're addressing us. However, it can be anything but difficult to dismiss that in our relationship or marriage since when you've been along with somebody for some time, you can get careless or even sluggish when it comes to giving them the total attention they merit.

Being present in your relationship is urgent to its prosperity as it permits you to be at the time with your partner. Not exclusively does being present affect your relationship's life span, but it impacts your satisfaction too. Being present gives you a degree of connection expected to grasp and perceive your love for another, and likewise to help remind you of the reasons in which you love this person.

Presence is the ability to show up and be there for somebody without embedding an individual plan. This implies allowing our gatekeeper to guard so we can give the other individual access. Presence can be difficult but fundamental expertise for successful relationships.

Loving presence plays a critical factor in offering emotional help to another. Analysts have just discovered that unsupportive behavior during a contention, such as making light of the significance of the problem, demanding after recommendations or offering spur of the moment advance, is a reliable indicator of future relationship distress.

Sometimes we have to talk about a problem without attempting to tackle it. A few problems can't be tackled. Sometimes we simply need somebody to hold our hand at the memorial service and rest in a seat close to us in the clinic bed. Sometimes we simply need to feel somewhat less alone and somewhat less apprehensive on the planet

The ability to focus on the present moment—or be with what is—without being judgmental or receptive is alluded to as mindfulness. Luckily for Dan, mindfulness is an ability that can be improved.

The term mindfulness initially originated from one factor of the Buddhist Noble Eightfold way. Still, otherworldly specialists everywhere throughout the world have been rehearsing the craft of being here now for centuries. Similarly, as competitors do physical activities without anyone else to turn out to be better at playing sports with others, mindfulness specialists build up their capacity to be present through yoga, reflection, thought, or qigong to be completely present with others.

Mindfulness practices include concentrating the mind on a solitary point, such as the breath, a melody, a sluggish movement, or even the perfect inside. When the mind strays (as it does), the expert mostly sees that and returns to the core interest point.

That is practically it, but these straightforward practices give a heap of mental and emotional advantages. Exploration contemplates showing that mindfulness helps for tension and sadness, chronic drug use, and even Borderline Personality Disorder. Mindfulness helps for relationships as well.

There's real artistry to embracing the here and now, and it's not as simple as it appears. There's continually another thing to contemplate, and that can genuinely remove us from the moment. Being present is significant in each part of life, but it very well may be especially significant when it goes to our romantic relationships

So how would you be more "there " when you're with your partner or spouse? You put forth a conscious attempt to remain completely present in their life and treat them with love and respect.

HERE ARE A FEW DIFFERENT WAYS TO DO THAT:

Always take a nice look at your partner. This necessary demonstration can help remind you of what attracted you to your partner in the first place. Take a look at one another; offer a moment where you're centered around each other. Look into your partner's spirit, and permit them to investigate yours. Eye to eye connection is the right type of closeness, try it out.

Set aside an effort to tune in to your partner. Try not to consider what you should state straight away, but be present and focus on the words being said. Sometimes it's the most straightforward motions that can help the individual over the room feel esteemed and heard.

Having alone time too is crucial. Focus on it to invest energy alone—merely you two, regardless of whether it's an end of the week escape, going through a day at the nearby historical center, or having a cookout at the recreation center, set aside an effort to grasp your love and commitment to each other.

Closeness comes in many shapes and sizes, but clasping hands while strolling down the road, embracing each other as you sit tight for the train, or essentially grinning from over the room, would all be able to be a significant type of closeness. It's a method to tell your partner that you're considering them and that you look for closeness.

Offer space, regardless of whether it's sharing a

home, sharing a taxi, or sharing your heart. Be respectful, be benevolent, and let your partner in. Permit yourself to be powerless. Permit yourself to trust. With self-introduction comes incredible connections. Opening up can sometimes be difficult, so do it when you're prepared, but know that your relationship's advantages will be gratifying.

A significant piece of being present is mindful. Be accommodating of your partner. Be mindful; know. Be cautious with the heart and feelings of your other half. Thinking about each other will likewise develop your bond and further fortify your relationship.

Focusing on someone else isn't just about a title or a ring—it's not just about having somebody call your individual. Commitment is tied in with being there for the defining moments, the tough situations, and the evenings with the sofa, a container of pizza, and Netflix. Appreciate the bond in which you have manufactured, and sustain it. Deal with love, all things considered, as effectively lost as it is found.

When your partner or spouse is talking to you, stop whatever else you're doing, and give them your full focus.

If your mind begins to wander when your partner or spouse is talking to you, look into their eyes, and feel the love you have. That will associate you to them in a significant manner, rather than underestimating them.

WHY ATTENTION IS IMPORTANT IN YOUR RELATIONSHIP

Things being what they are, why do we give such a vast amount of significance to attention in a relationship? Is focusing on detail in relationships that important all things considered? Indeed, it is! Also, in light of current circumstances as well!

You most likely think the entire world is in the center, similar to a photo. It isn't. Spot your finger a couple of inches from here, center around it, and attempt to peruse the following sentence. You can't. The fovea, the focal point of the eye, is a little locale where we see forcefully, and the mind imagines that the rest is in the center also. Attention is that way, as well. Consider it an electric lamp or a light if you're British. You just observe what it is pointing at.

We frequently swing it fiercely around, as though we are in timberland on a moonless night, checking for branches, gullies, predators, and prey. What's more, we're not entirely in charge of it either, as any individual who has attempted to contemplate will bear witness to. It seems as though another person likewise has hold of the electric lamp handle, and continues taking command.

Our language mirrors this nonstop difference in the center. "My attention was gotten by... ." "Let me cause you to notice... ." "Focus!"

That is, from numerous points of view, something worth being thankful for. The smoke caution demands attention in any event when immersed in "Round of Thrones," similarly as we see movement in our fringe vision.

What's more, what we focus on isn't just occasions in the outside world; it's frequently inside. The past or the future engrossed us, and we changed our attention to our faculties sufficiently only to abstain from strolling into the furnishings.

Presently apply this to your relationships with others, regardless of whether colleagues or your lover. If you're not focusing, you won't see them. If you're consistently exchanging attention, you will just observe them a bit. When you give them your complete attention, they become, for that time, your whole world. You recognize the truth about them, however, obviously separated by your beliefs and biases. What's more, this other individual, regardless of whether a checkout assistant or your lover, can feel your look, will react to your attention, because our responses are a lot social.

It is just through attention that a relationship exists by any means. If you give no attention, that individual doesn't exist for you. When you stroll with somebody, you focus on pace and bearing, in case you become two separate bodies in the group; thus, it is in a relationship: it is your precise attention to one another that holds it together and makes it genuine.

When that attention becomes shared complete attention, a sacred space is made, that unique method of being together that we have as of late expounded on. By not focusing on past occasions or future concerns, you can be present to yourself and your partner. When your mind isn't topped off with concerns and your attention isn't coordinated somewhere else, you will experience the enchantment and totality of association with another.

Toward the day's end, the whole custom of being a couple is justified, despite all the trouble when you both feel the love for one another. If that is feeling the loss, the ceremonial beginnings are getting useless, and the relationship begins to bite the dust. Sometimes it's the start of the end, and sometimes it is the warning which when paid attention to resuscitates a relationship.

There are billions of us, and our lives could become mixed up in that disarray, but the way that our partner sees our lives, records it, lives it with us makes the entire thing beneficial. It likewise props the communication in a relationship up.

All in all, if in the midst of all that you feel like you're not getting enough attention from your sweetheart, what's even the point? So if you feel that you can't concentrate on your partner, he is things you ought to do.

HOW TO GIVE YOUR PARTNER THE NEEDED ATTENTION

Learn How to Listen. Listening is more than hearing. It's body language, head gesturing, posing questions, focusing (not being on your telephone), and showing you are occupied with the conversation. At that point, it's making what you heard one stride farther and following up on your conversation. Being a decent audience can transform a healthy relationship into a tremendous one.

Asking questions is a primary method to be more mindful. Get some information about their day.

Inquire as to whether they need anything when you get up to go to the kitchen. Ask how they're feeling. Ask how their clubs or employment are going. Inquire as to whether they talked to their family. Simply pose questions that show you're focusing and that you're keen on their lives.

Accomplishing something they've always wanted to do is another way to give your partner the much-needed attention. Possibly they've for the longest time been itching to go to the zoo to take care of the giraffes or visit the neighborhood craft exhibition hall that everybody raves about. Whatever it is, treat them to it! Cause them to feel unique since they are!

Achieve more things together. If you're an exercise center rodent, but your partner's a city sprinter, pick a day when they run with you, and you go to the recreation center with them. Check whether you can press get-togethers into your day. The additional time you spend together, the more possibilities you must be mindful, to show enthusiasm, to be affectionate, and to become acquainted with your partner shockingly better.

Bedroom Attention is also quite important. Get some attractive new underwear or a fun new toy and let them know you're prepared to joy them! There's nothing hotter than being mindful in the room, and your partner will thank you for it.

To meet your partner's needs you also need to focus on their body. Tune in to their breathing and focus on their body movements when you engage in sexual relations. Notice when they get a hairstyle. Contribute somewhat more when you notice they're feeling depleted or wiped out. Show care and concern when they limp. Have a delicate and thinking about their disposition and body.

Chances are if your partner could utilize some attention; at that point, a little gift will go far. Snatch their preferred container of Scotch or wine, or get them a gift card to their preferred store. This little signal will show that you're pondering them, regardless of whether you've been excessively occupied of late.

There's no reason for overlooking commemorations, birthday celebrations, and unique events. You can place the dates into your telephone and get vast amounts of reminders. Go a bit farther and put in different exceptional events, similar to a year at their particular employment, the commemoration of when you got you ahead of everyone else, or their preferred pet's birthday.

Getting into your spouse's Interests is also quite

important towards meeting his or her needs.If you despise sports, you don't need to become a fan out of nowhere, but you may think it's enjoyable to go to a game together or have a close following get-together. If there's a show they like, watch it as well, so you can talk about it. Learn about what they love so you can pose questions or get them things they may require. It will go far to help your partner to feel known and understood.

SOLUTIONS FOR THE LACK OF ATTENTION TO YOUR RELATIONSHIP

When speaking with your partner, ensure you have your partner's complete attention. This implies not expecting your partner is listening since you're talking. Instead, check-in: "Is this a decent time to talk ?" Especially if it is important to you or the relationship. If you, as the audience, are centered around something, and your partner starts talking, you can repeat and state, "I truly need to hear what you're stating, and I'm engaged/diverted by this. Would I be able to wrap this up extremely snappy and afterward talk to you about this? I need to give you your complete attention, and I'm diverted at this moment." FYI, if you settle on an agreement like this but don't finish, your partner won't trust your statement. So finish. Remember, both the speaker and the audience have duties in keeping the conversation spotless and bright.

If your relationship is devoured by heftiness, plunk down with your partner and investigate how your time is spent. Check whether there are little chances to set aside a few minutes for emotional connection. I have proposed a few ceremonies here: 7 Daily Rituals Intentional Couples Use to Cultivate Lasting Love.

For attention weakness when it comes to stress, I would recommend having a day by day stress decreasing conversation, just as planning a State of the Union gathering when the two partners have vitality so you can hear each other and stir together to think of a solution.

If gadgets are a problem, read this article: Four Common Solvable Problems in Relationships. Gadgets have become a significant problem in my life. Hence, I read Digital Minimalism and experienced an attention diet. Knowing that my attention is constrained, I need to ensure I center it around essentials most in my life.

Keep records of another experience with one another. Frequently in relationships with kids, the youngsters get a wide range of new exercises while the grown-ups get the daily schedule of the day by day life. Get the innocent interest and perkiness into your relationship. Investigate new pieces of one another when you take a stab at moving, painting, another exercise class, wine sampling, or even better approaches for communicating love, and so on.

Attention is the essential food and water of a living and breathing relationship. Attention is how we support and feed. Attention is what we require and pine for. Without attention, no relationship, regardless of how solid, can get by for long—the underlying foundations of connection just psychologist and whither. Attention is the most fundamental type of love. Through it, we favor and are honored.

So now, while you, despite everything, can, while we're as yet capable, go love your love, focus on him, touch her cheek. Look into his eyes. Get some information about her work. Ask him how his mom is. Try not to pause. Life is short, and time swiftly cruises by.

Love and life are complicated and testing. Furthermore, hence, it's essential to devote the little moments we have to the most critical relationship of our lives.

6

DISAGREEMENTS ARE NORMAL AMONGST EACH OTHER

Quarrels and fights are important to keep a developing relationship more beneficial. Every other couple now and then engages in quarrels. If somebody has never battled with his spouse, then he has unquestionably missed one fascinating part of his purported developed relationship. Fights followed by a progression of influence and different methods for inducement hold particular importance for a relationship. Many times such little fights lead to frivolous conflicts which later gets forgotten about by the couple and at different times it very well may be justified to show up at a typical agreement. In such cases, it's smarter to just settle on a truce. This is what's standard out of a developing relationship regardless of whether there emerges some difference in the thoughts.

The conflicting thoughts for a couple aren't something exceptionally remarkable. It surely can't be that one be the equal representation of his spouse when talking about thoughts or suppositions. Everybody has their personality and uniqueness, the opportunity of thought fluctuates from individual to individual. It doesn't make a difference if the concerned people are as of now in a developing relationship; arguments will undoubtedly happen when there is a difference in conclusion over a specific subject.

It's a confusion of the people, which causes them to believe that couples associated with a developing relationship ought never to have any disagreements whatsoever. A young couple feels their romantic connection is to keep going forever, so they get off watched after confronting any circumstances like minor fights or warmed arguments. This way, both the spouses shroud their feelings to keep away from such a quarrel. They might be directly in their specific manners, but the inquiry is if theirs is an adult relationship, will it get influenced by any argument or disagreement.

Conflict in a relationship might be characterized

as any sort of disagreement, including an argument, or a progressing arrangement of disagreements, for instance, about how to go through cash. Strife can be amazingly stressful, but it can likewise act to 'eliminate any confusion air', surfacing issues that need conversation.

Conflicts and disagreements may bring about us losing control, and they may likewise emerge because we have lost control over something different. At work, we may attempt to control our outrage and abstain from making statements we may lament. At home, lamentably, we are considerably more prone to direct frightful sentiments toward others thus. There are additionally more reluctant to be others around who can intercede, and disagreements along these lines rapidly heighten in a manner that probably won't occur at work.

This implies struggle in a relationship can quickly turn out to be terrible, and extremely close to home.

Unfortunately, when we are near people, we regularly know how best to hurt them. Out of frustration, that might be actually what we need to do, however much we think twice about it later.

If you're similar to many people, when you think you are correct and your partner isn't right - you may not say the words, 'You're off-base!" - but your signals and manner of speaking might be quite obvious. How may you handle this differently? Why might you need to?

Have you at any point heard the adage, 'Would you like to be correct or would you like to be hitched?' There is a ton of insight into this platitude. The more you think your partner isn't right, the more you tell your partner they're off-base or utilize related motions or manner of speaking, the more you harm your relationship and lessen the odds of connection, respect, trust, and closeness. Doesn't sound so great, isn't that right?

One of the most important intentions for helping keep a healthy relationship is to 'move in the direction of' your partner, particularly when you would prefer not to. What does 'move in the direction of' mean?

HOW HAPPY COUPLES DEAL WITH DISAGREEMENTS

Every couple differs from one another. The impeccable similarity is beyond the realm of imagination, but reasonably working; however, inconsistency is. The difference between a happy couple and a troubled couple is how they handle their disagreements. Consequently, to become and be successful in our connections, we should embrace sound adapting procedures for managing our differences.

The following are the absolute best strategies cheerful couples handle disagreements:

They attack their disagreements, not one another. Disagreements are beautiful, and arguments are as well. These are characteristic, centered responses to an individual's choices or behavior. But when disagreements and arguments snowball into worldwide assaults on the other individual, and not on their choices or behavior, this means something is wrong. For instance: "They didn't call me when they said they would because they overlooked, but because they're a repulsive, pathetic, abhorrent individual."

In any event, when it's challenging to think obviously without giving it much thought, you need to take a full breath and remember that your partner is in your group. Continuously support each other, in any event, when you disagree. Try not to take your stress out on one another. Maintain your emphasis on the problematic disagreement and it together by talking it out and arriving at a compromise.

Both parties taking responsibility shows how

mature couples can be with conflicts in their relationships. When you refuse to take responsibility in each relationship disagreement, all you're truly doing is accusing your partner. You're stating, as a result, "The problem is never me, it's consistently you." This forswearing of responsibility just heightens the argument, because there's a complete breakdown of communication.

So assume liability for your activities. Assume liability for your relationship – the great times and the terrible. Work with your partner. Communicate. Accusing them is a copout that achieves nothing. It is possible that you both take equivalent responsibility for problems both of you experience together, or the problems will possess both of you.

Happy couples also practice purposeful communication amidst conflicts. Your partner isn't a mind reader. Offer your musings openly. Give them the information they need as opposed to anticipating that they should know everything. The more that remaining parts are implicit, the more noteworthy the hazard for problems. Begin imparting plainly. Try not to attempt to guess what they might be thinking, and don't attempt to peruse yours. Most problems, of all shapes and sizes, inside a relationship, start with broken communication.

Likewise, don't tune in so you can answer – tune in to understand. Open your ears and mind to your partner's interests and assessments without judgment. Take a gander at things from your partner's point of view just as your own. Attempt to imagine their perspective. Regardless of whether you don't understand precisely where they're coming from, you can, in any case, respect them. So turn your body towards them, look at them without flinching, turn off the PC, and set aside your telephone. Doing so exhibits that you need to communicate with your partner and hear what they need to state; this fortifies such a supportive environment that is pivotal for compromise.

They are happy to make sacrifices for one another. The most joyful private bonds are attached with true love, and true love includes attention, mindfulness, control, exertion, and having the option to think about somebody and sacrifice for them, always, in endless negligible, little, unsexy ways consistently. You put your arms around them and love them notwithstanding, in any event, when they do not see things your way. Also, they do likewise for you.

If you genuinely need to know what a cheerful, stable relationship is, it's one where two people get up each morning and state, "This is justified, despite all the trouble. You are justified, despite all the trouble. I am cheerful you are in my life." It's about real sacrifice. It's tied in with knowing that a few days you should do things you hate to make the one you love to grin, and feeling completely enchanted to do as such.

One other way is that happy couples are focused on managing disagreements, decidedly. Frequently it very well may be least demanding to run from a disagreement, particularly if you're not a fierce individual necessarily. But remember, this isn't about you or whether you feel like managing your differences. It's about what your relationship needs to develop and flourish over the long haul; so put these needs in front of your own. The two partners must be focused on managing their disagreements, since running from them will just make matters more difficult to manage not far off.

One of the best instruments couples can use to facilitate the way toward managing disagreements is utilizing positive language. Relationships prosper when the two people can share their deepest feelings and contemplations positively. One viable technique for doing this during an argument is to give a valiant effort to abstain from utilizing "you" and attempt to utilize "I." This makes it a lot simpler to communicate feelings and a lot harder to the other individual incidentally.

The establishment of love is to let those we care about be proudly themselves and not to misshape them to accommodate our vain thoughts of who they ought to be. Else we begin to look all starry eyed at just with our dreams, and in this manner pass up a great opportunity totally on their true excellence. So spare your relationship from unnecessary stress. Rather than attempting to change your partner, give them your support and become together, as people.

Each marriage has struggled too, which is why knowing how to communicate with your spouse is so important.

There are many zones in a marriage where you're just not going to concur. Here is a couple:

- One of you wants to have kids (or X number of children), while different says they're not prepared or are content with the current number of children.
- One of you wants sex unquestionably more regularly than the other.
- You need to bring up your kids Baptist,

> while your spouse wants them to be
> raised Catholic.

- Your spouse is remiss about housework and once in a while does their offer until you annoy, touching off outrage.
- One of you is a saver with cash and the other is a high-roller.
- Or one of you wants to progress in the direction of a more straightforward and moderate sort of life, and the other doesn't.

Problems in marriage are unavoidable. The inquiry is — would you be able to stay fulfilled in your marriage regardless of differences? Will your marriage flourish when there are differences between you?

The key is to work it out and grow up persistently. Acknowledge the problem and talk about it. Your love for one another doesn't need to be over-powered by your differences.

In shaky marriages, elephants are probably going to murder the relationship. Rather than adapting, the couple gets gridlocked. You have a similar conversation, again and again, settling nothing. You're wasting your time. Also, since you're gaining no ground, you both feel more disappointed, hurt, or dismissed. When this occurs, resentment moves in and humor and affection leave – as well as effortlessness and enthusiasm.

Problems in marriage will occur. How you address them is up to you; in this way, this takes us to how to best communicate with your partner during arguments and disagreements.

HOW TO COMMUNICATE WITH YOUR PARTNER WHEN YOU DISAGREE

The first way is to plainly define yourself. To characterize yourself implies you have more profound mindfulness and understanding of your beliefs, wants, needs, and wants. Marriage is an incredible spot to clarify these things in your life – for the most part since that is how marriage is structured.

You live with someone else who has their perspective on how things ought to be, much the same as you. For instance, in your group of a starting point, tables may fill in as extraordinary spots to store heaps of mail, magazines, and the child's beautiful art. But your spouse's group of starting points believes tables are incredible spots to have supper together, so they should be liberated from a mess.

Neither one of these ways is fundamentally "right," merely different. You are permitted to live life how you pick, but so is your spouse.

To experience effective communication with your spouse, treating your spouse with respect is quite crucial. One of the first things I find in couples nearly marital breakdown is an absence of respect. When you arrive at a point where you do not, at this point like one another, you're in a tough situation.

Unfortunately, we frequently treat regular outsiders with more respect than people in our home. Respect is one of the key elements to a successful and upbeat marriage — respect for everyone around you, and most importantly, respect for yourself.

Talk before you are irate and concur with a procedure. Managing strife requires a commitment from both of you. Talk heretofore about how you might want to manage disagreements, and concur that you will help each other.

You may think that it's helpful to talk about how you carry on when you are furious, and support each other to manage that. For instance, if one of you loses control rapidly, it might be helpful for the other to propose holding until some other time to talk.

Consistent apology is another thing. You may

feel that you were morally justified. You may even have been morally justified.

Being set up to apologize for the way that your partner feels, however, will go far towards guaranteeing that they feel they have been heard, and that you understand their interests. This is particularly true if, despite your best goals, you wound up yelling at one another.

Saying 'sorry' doesn't mean you need to acknowledge that you weren't right.

It implies saying that you are heartbroken that there was a disagreement, and you are grieved that your partner is vexed and that you are focused on finding a route forward that works for you both.

A difference of supposition or any minor fight is required for a decent and developed relationship as it encourages the couple to become acclimated to the sentiments and behaviors of their partners. But it ought to likewise be remembered that the disagreements ought to be taken with a positive temper, it ought not to insult your partner nor should you feel annoyed by the restriction. You need not be quiet when you feel you have a different conclusion with your partner; you can feel free to tell him what your contemplations are. A minor disagreement followed by a legitimate conversation lastly excusing the differences is the indication of a developing relationship.

In any case, don't begin fighting with your partner to term it as a developed relationship if you have genuinely nothing to grumble and you share similar suppositions with your partner. Learning to have substantial disagreements will permit your growing dating relationship to go higher than ever. It's when the disagreement grows into a destructive fight that it isn't acceptable. Keep things non-emotional and permit each other to voice their conclusion and feelings. You would prefer the honesty of this sort of relationship than the trickery of whatever else. Developing a dating relationship is based on two people who know how to fight well.

7

DO SOMETHING NICE FOR YOUR PARTNER

It's convenient to take for granted the person you're nearest to and who cares about so much. The deep intimacy that an intimate bond brings with it ensures that you feel so relaxed with your partner that you don't feel like you have to breathe air. Such airs may also be helpful, though, because it means that you show your partner the same compassion that you would show to a stranger. You wouldn't interrupt someone you don't know very well, be critical, use rough language, or be intrusive and intrusive. You dress up whenever you meet someone for the first time and listen to your appearance so that you can be viewed in a socially appropriate way. Why, then, do you think you can violate the social niceties with your partner?

Research on happy couples proposes that having the option to show your actual self contributes to a decent relationship as it mirrors the closeness of your feelings. However, there might be limits to precisely how much you should toss aside the standards of social show. For instance, if you're feeling horrible because of something that occurred at work, is it a smart thought to let your disappointments out on your partner? If you went through the entire day stifling your annoyance toward your chief or associates, why is it at that point alright to vent the entirety of that obnoxiousness out on the individual who you love, and who loves you?

In this way, treating your partner with as much sagacity as you treat your associates, or others as a rule, is by all accounts advantageous in managing this key region of a couple's relationship.

We can utilize these 10 tips on how to be a nicer individual with the individual you love the most:

WAYS YOU CAN START BEING NICER TO THE ONE YOU LOVE

Put forth an attempt to understand your partner's needs. Political aptitude, as shown via Carnes, helps men, at any rate, coexist better with their partners to the extent that conflict can take away from a couple's fulfillment. Taking a page from the political abilities playbook implies that you take a gander at your relationship with your partner as worth your time and vitality.

To respect your partner's feelings, you have to respect your partner's limits. You could never rudely request that a colleague share exceptionally close to home subtleties. Your partner may have a few territories that the person in question wishes to keep hidden. Try not to go where you're not welcomed.

There is no motivation to be inconsiderate or vulgar with your partner, despite the fact that you feel that you can act naturally."Keep up probably a portion of the decent behaviors with your partner that you would when you're out of the house, including social graces and by and large disposition. Be cautious with the words you use. That political ability file included social sagacity, or knowing the correct comments to other people. You don't need to alter yourself very vigorously in your nearest relationships, but it's as yet important to express your communication such that it isn't terrible or disrespectful.

Recollect that the relationship is a two-way road. You might want to, and most likely to be sure expect, that your partner will treat you with graciousness and respect. Once more, coming back to the idea of political expertise, some portion of coexisting with others is having the option to see yourself comparable to them. How would you need your partner to see you? Probably, you want to be treated with thoughtfulness and a smidgen of graciousness, and in this way, you ought to show a similar degree of consideration.

To be nice to your partner, you have to know that your partner might be as stressed as you seem to be. Work-family conflict as far as job commitments and over-burden are genuine contenders with your capacity to make the most of your partner. It might feel normal to consider yourself the stressed-out one, but it's conceivable your partner gets back home with a comparative degree of tension. If you can be a sounding board for your partner's disappointment, this can go far toward both of you feeling ready to take the outside world. It doesn't hurt to offer help on days or weeks that are especially stressful for your partner.

Try not to make suspicions about what your partner is feeling. That social mindfulness Carnes contemplated incorporates having the option to read people well, and to do this, you have to keep up a receptive outlook toward what others are encountering. You wouldn't profess to know what an outsider is thinking, and despite the fact that you know your partner well indeed, be fit to be shocked at what you realize.

It's extraordinary to feel that you don't need to put your open face on while at home, but from time to time your partner may value you getting spruced up, regardless of whether it's only an apathetic Sunday evening. It's especially important that you do as such if the Sunday evening incorporates a visit from your partner's family. Showing respect to the others your partner thinks about might be similarly as important as showing you care about how your partner sees you.

Always expecting your partner to be honest, which is also another nice gesture you can show to your partner. Is it accurate to say that you are suspicious of what your partner is doing when you're not together, or do you feel that your partner sometimes conceals for a mix-up or for spending a lot on garments? This causes it difficult for your partner to feel acknowledged and can prompt your being seen as conniving yourself.

Stop yourself before you state something you'll wish you could reclaim. When a few words are stated, they can't be implied, despite the fact that it's simpler to apologize to your partner than to somebody you don't know that well. All things considered, if you practice your political aptitudes in the home, you'll abstain from making an excessive number of those inappropriate or excessively unforgiving comments.

COMPLIMENT YOUR PARTNER

A pleasant utterance of applause and profound respect one regularly terms as 'compliment' appears to leave stock once wedded. Prior to marriage, there's no deficiency, in reality the stock is unlimited. At that point why did the lack once hitched?

Among many things one underestimates in a marriage, extraction of compliments is one of them – compliments not just stop to pour, they stop to sprinkle through and through. Marriage, particularly in our nation appears to give permission to underestimate one another. When couples change or quit concentrating on the better subtleties like showering compliments, offering love and thanks, they once used to, one may feel one's partner has changed – in spite of the fact that they naturally continue as before.

Because one is hitched doesn't mean one gets careless with things. A couple may quit complimenting one another, but the moment a third individual showers a few compliments, they feel euphoric. How unexpected! It's human to feel cheerful when complimented. All relationships develop through compliments - extra-conjugal included. Henceforth when couples having experienced it with one another, stop the training once wedded, feel at the head of the world when complemented by a pariah.

Compliments can have a positive influence on your marriage. When you offer genuine encouragement and compliments to your spouse, a few things occur. Your spouse's self-assurance increments, just as your own self-esteem. The companionship among you is reinforced and you make an upbeat moment for you two to share. When you offer your spouse a compliment, you show your thankfulness and cause them to feel esteemed and esteemed. You likewise center around the positive rather than the negative, which is something each marriage needs.

THE DIFFERENCE BETWEEN FLATTERY AND COMPLIMENTS

It is important that your compliments are true and legitimate. When they aren't, your comments transform into adulation, which is false or dishonest applause. Sweet talk is typically received with cynicism and is regularly seen as being manipulative. As it were, sweet words are frequently simply used to get something you need from the individual you are complimenting. It is about you, not them. A genuine compliment is said with the center reason to cause another person to feel great.

Probably the greatest effect of compliments is that it strengthens behavior. So if there is something you compliment, it is probably going to get your spouse to do it more. Respected marriage analyst, Dr. John Gottman, attests that in great marriages, compliments (and great connections when all is said in done) need to dwarf reactions by at any rate five to one. Fortunately, if you are low on your reminder, it's a simple fix.

TIPS FOR COMPLIMENTING YOUR SPOUSE

- Use "I" rather than "you." For example, state, "I welcome that you cleaned the house" rather than "You worked superbly cleaning the house."
- Use consistent non-verbal communication when you compliment. Grin, look and talk in a warm and genuine manner.
- Be specific. For instance, it's smarter to state "That shading draws out your beautiful eyes" as opposed to "You look beautiful."
- Compliment your spouse's character too. Comment on your spouse's pleasantness, insight, consideration, and enormous heart.
- If you are the beneficiary of a compliment, take it in generous. Try not to act naturally censuring or deny your partner's point of view on something positive or great.
- Don't have a concealed plan or camouflage your compliment in an

analysis. Your compliments must be immediate and earnest. Try not to state, "I'm happy you are at long last on time." Say, "I love that you showed up so expeditiously."

At last, keeping the parity on the positive side of the relationship is only a consistent stream of little demonstrations of love. Sure a terrific motion is nice now and again, but it's the easily overlooked details that truly matter. Try not to avoid those day by day compliments; they'll wind up being the magic that binds everything.

MAKE YOUR SPOUSE FEEL SPECIAL AGAIN

Focusing on your spouse to feel special and among your many relationships is an important and deliberate decision that takes work. However, this is the most important work that will serve to keep your family solid and stable.

Always Keep up the "Enchantment" in Marriage. Continue saying "I love you." These three little words are amazing! Barely any people, if any, feel worn out on hearing that they are loved. When you state "I love you" give a valiant effort to be giving your spouse your complete consideration. Ensure you mean it when you state it!!

Give veritable, important assertions normally. "Well, your hair smells terrific" might be fitting, but assertions as "You accomplish such a great deal to keep our family working. I can never thank you enough for everything you do" are all the more impressive and important for causing your spouse to feel special. Certifications come in all shapes and sizes: from verbal attestations given face to face, to phone message or email messages to notes and cards.

Getting away together is another way to make him or her feel special. Same thought as the customary night out on the town noted previously. An excursion with your spouse will give you more opportunity to concentrate on each other and will give you chances to revive the romance in your life!

To make your partner feel special, surprise your spouse once in a while. For instance, seize your spouse from work and accomplish something you know they would appreciate. (Make certain to check with your spouse's chief – if they have one!) Give gifts or roses at absolutely surprising times.

Purchase your spouse roses or gifts. Gifts don't need to be excessive, but ought to be basic tokens of how special your spouse is to you. Keep these gifts individual, as opposed to handy!

If you travel, attempt to communicate with your spouse regularly while you are away. Calls are ideal, trailed by voice messages and messages. If you need to keep your spouse feeling special, don't offer remarks like "This is the best time I've at any point had in my life" regardless of whether it is. "I truly miss you" works much better!

GIFTING- A GOOD WAY TO BE NICE TO YOUR PARTNER

Gifts have consistently been an important part whenever you wish to build up a solid and loving relationship. This is because gifts will in general offer various advantages planned for causing your relationship to get more grounded and keep going forever. While most relationships are novel in their own particular manner, it's not possible for anyone to deny the effect that gifts have when it comes to making a more grounded bond and keeping up further connections with each other. If you are still in question on whether to get her or him a neckband or some other gift, here are a portion of the upsides of gift-giving that will make you alter your perspective totally.

Gifting builds your reputation. From the moment you choose to begin dating truly, your social notoriety will consistently be out of your hands. This is because most women will in general offer nearly everything with their companions who in the end share with their sweethearts. In this manner, a gift once in a while can go far in building your notoriety since they are generally connected with well-meaning goals. You ought to consider offering a gift on occasion if you need to keep yourself in great books with each and every individual who partners with the individual that you are dating.

There is appreciation in gifting as well. In a relationship, it is in every case better to help your significant other to remember how you love and welcome them now and again. With a gift, you can accomplish this without fundamentally starting to perspire. This is because it will in general delineate how you give it a second thought and value their quality in your life. To cause your partner to feel your love, you can either choose to go with an ordinary gift or a romantic one as Testo Drive 365, it will in any case work.

Gift-giving is a demonstration that has consistently been in existence since prehistoric times. However, you ought not to stretch yourself as far as possible if you are to offer the ideal gift as it will just cause you to feel stressed. Regardless of whether you are searching for gifts for her or him, you need to recall that the easiest things in life, when offered with love and care, will consistently be the ideal gift. Put forth an attempt to give your loved one and perceive how your relationship is going to improve.

Coexisting with your partner necessitates that both of you explore and haggle some exceptionally close to home and difficult regions. Rehearsing niceness can help make your important relationships significantly more satisfying and agreeable for both of you.

8

SET ASIDE TIME TO TALK

We all know that talking to your partner and being open about your feelings is important. But it tends to be shockingly simple to let making time to consistently talk fall by the wayside — especially with the demands of a bustling working life or caring for youngsters.

You've most likely heard that communication is one of the keys to a perfect relationship, but that is frequently more difficult than one might expect. Now and again, communication in a relationship can be out and out hard. Two people with different characters can battle to communicate in a compelling and solid manner. However, if you need your relationship to last, it's important to take a shot at figuring out how to talk to your partner to improve your relationship.

THE IMPORTANCE OF IMPROVING YOUR COMMUNICATION

Studies have discovered that having positive and great communication can be a pointer of the satisfaction of a couple. If you communicate well with your beau, at that point this is uplifting news. But, many couples battle here. What's more, as per one survey of mental wellbeing experts, helpless communication is the main source of couples separating.

It is a typical misinterpretation that you must have a comparative communication style as your partner all together for your relationship to succeed. While it might be all the more testing to get familiar with another method of communication, it positively doesn't block you from having the option to take a shot at issues with your sweetheart. If this is the situation in your relationship, both you and your sweetheart must have the option to oblige each other by understanding that their style may be different but it is right. Besides, the manner in which you give love probably won't be the manner in which you need to receive love. If you don't think you and your sweetheart have great communication aptitudes at this moment, don't stress. Your relationship isn't damned. It's been discovered that couples can improve the joy of their relationship by learning better communication abilities.

Why is talking each day important? A couple of reasons - Firstly, it permits you to talk about whatever may be irritating you. Having the space to go over whatever you may be finding difficult — either in the relationship or in life by and large — implies you'll have the option to communicate and cooperate to address the problem.

Without doing this, things can aggregate and make pressure. It very well may be enticing to just attempt to hide things away from plain view to keep the harmony. But building up a capacity to talk things over in a positive and gainful manner (and without the conversation transforming into an argument) implies you'll have the option to change in accordance with the inescapable difficulties that will come your way during your time as a couple.

Conveying along these lines is an ability that comes more normally to certain people than others, and it very well may be difficult to begin if you haven't had a lot of training. But you can learn. If you'd like tips on talking, look at our communication tips to attempt with your partner. This short rundown of thoughts will help you to communicate in a manner that is bound to prompt understanding.

Furthermore, talking standard is important, because it's additionally just an incredible method of feeling near each other. Indeed, it's probably the most ideal approach to feel associated with your partner.

Talking together doesn't need to mean going over huge stuff — sometimes it can simply mean staying nearby together and appreciating each other's conversation. It can mean sharing a joke, talking about how the day has gone or making arrangements for the end of the week.

What's important is that you're getting to know one another, without interference, to be close, and basically appreciate being in a couple.

WHY COUPLES SHOULD BE TALKING ABOUT THEIR FEELINGS

As a couple, you're constantly talking about what's for dinner and plans with friends or family. The day-to-day running of your lives together, particularly if you have kids,[1] is often the central focus of your conversations. Talking about these things is necessary, but the most important piece that you should not gloss over is how you feel about what's going on in your life day-to-day.

These more profound conversations are important to make the "stick" that holds you together and makes the closeness people want in their marriage. It's important that you talk about your highs and lows that have been sprinkled consistently. These themes might be from outside associations with others or something specifically among you and your spouse.

The two women and men can battle with sharing feelings, but men appear to have a much harder time. Spouses every now and again grumble about the "absence of closeness" or "connection" with their husbands. What's more, for women, closeness and connection are what starts her sexual want. In this manner, it merits the exertion, folks!

The perks of constant communication between couples are so numerous and they include: keep fights from heightening, prevent hatred among couples, helps your partner feel compassion and "stroll from your point of view", set off holding hormones, create a profound and important connection with your partner, get out of having just shallow conversations and to mention a few.

Don't simply concentrate on the realities, but

likewise center around how you feel about the responses to these questions. What comes up as you are talking about it with your spouse? Would you be able to identify a specific feeling, for example, shock, satisfaction, sadness,3 outrage? How about the harder ones like dismissal, disgrace, or embarrassment?

If you are uncertain, it's alright to state that you don't know how you feel. It's alright to check whether your partners, who may have all the more a "language" for feelings, help you out. You can feel befuddled or have blended emotions as well. Whatever it is, put forth a valiant effort to portray it.

There are some things you can do if you struggle with talking about deeper topics with your partner. A few people truly battle to raise the points that sway their relationship. This is because it takes advantage of our most exceedingly awful fears about being rejected, deserted or some other loathsome activity by our partner. But, similar to the regular daily existence points, it's insufficient to simply talk about your contemplations and assessments on the harder issues (child rearing, sex, parents in law, funds, etc.). You should likewise examine (you got it!) how you feel about these themes.

When one partner is receptive or avoidant about

proposing one of these subjects it is frequently demonstrative of something more profound. Couples must slice through preventing, raising outrage, or closing down to talk about their basic "center" emotions.

The more profound, center emotions are what keeps a profound and significant connection and romantic bond flourishing. It likewise forestalls on-going negative examples of communication. For example, if you feel "I can never satisfy her" or "I'm not important to him," this might be what sets one of you off into reactivity over your differing perspectives things like how to go through your cash, recurrence of sex or the measure of time went through with the parents in law.

It is substantially more gainful to communicate genuine feelings as opposed to giving the quiet treatment, conveying resentment, getting latent forceful, or hollering. Moreover, it is a lot simpler for your partner to react to these center delicate emotions. It is a success win for you both.

TIPS FOR MAKING DAILY CONVERSATIONS WITH YOUR PARTNER NEW AGAIN

When you fantasize about being in the ideal long haul relationship, we're willing to wager that the piece of the intrigue is in its conviction that all is good and scheduled. You relish the idea of returning home every day to the equivalent great individual, knowing that you'll have somebody to impart a dinner to, of the solace of somebody you love lying close to you in bed each night. It's practically the most ideal sort of schedule, no? But what happens when the consistency you once wanted for begins to feel somewhat stale? Of course, you get the opportunity to sit over the table from a similar individual consistently, but you likewise may start to feel like you're having a similar conversation with that individual consistently.

Regardless of whether the topic is only workplace issues and tasks, we searched out tips from communication and relationship specialists to cause your exhausting conversations with your spouse unexpectedly to feel new and fascinating once more.

You can start by always welcoming specific conversations. Measure what your special somebody really wants to talk about by essentially asking them!

Asking, "Do you have to talk about... ?" is an extraordinary spot to begin. "Any open-finished greeting to be heard sends the message that you are thought about and that you matter," energizes clergyman and psychotherapist Sheri Heller. "Offering quality time to tune in to your partner's musings and feelings extends your connection."

Another way is to always allow and make use of open-ended questions.Stay away from yes-or-no questions to keep the conversation streaming. Advisor Heidi McBain recommends a couple of model open-finished questions: What did you do at the beginning of today grinding away? Where did you go for lunch? What was the feature of your day? How did your early evening time meeting go?

Offer the great and the awful. Present the happenings of your day by arranging the high and depressed spots. At that point, welcome your S.O. to do likewise. Couples advocate and Baltimore Therapy Center chief Raffi Bilek noticed that surrounding your conversation along these lines should make for a more fascinating conversation than endeavoring to summarize your entire day in a solitary sudden spike in demand for sentence.

During important conversations, endeavor to keep your phone aside. This ought to be an easy decision regardless of who you're talking to, but if you truly need to associate with your significant other in the wake of a difficult day, authorized marriage and family specialist Melissa Dumaz fortifies the significance of unplugging. There are sufficient expected interruptions impacting everything during the weekday — don't acquaint superfluous ones by attempting to perform multiple tasks between talking to your partner what's more, following notifications.

React in the manner in which you would need to be reacted to. Keep the Golden Rule of conversations. "If you react all the more insightfully and intricately, you'll likely get more conversation from your spouse, too," reminds sex and relationship mentor Colby Marie. "As humans, we frequently mirror the sum and level of self-revelation from those we speak with, so if you give a great deal of data, your partner is bound to, also."

Would you like to make a more extravagant connection with your partner? To have those conversations that are cozy and significant? Is it accurate to say that you are closing down open doors for a more profound relationship with somebody you love by the manner in which you talk with them?

Pause, I'm grieved. Let me attempt those questions once more.

How to improve people? Relate a time when you had an important conversation. What sorts of questions evoke a more profound engagement?

HOW TO HAVE BETTER CONVERSATIONS WITH YOUR PARTNER

Everyone has conversations with people who are not gifted in associating, and perhaps we battle to interface in conversations. Associating through conversation is indispensable to any relationship, and our questions regularly decide the nature of that engagement. The way to pose drawing in inquiries might be easier than you might suspect.

There's an informal articulation: it's not what you state, but how you state it. Despite the fact that the tone of our questions is important, the genuine questions themselves are the way to connecting with conversations. Peruse the main section of this article once more. How would someone be able to react to the questions in this first section? They are totally shut ended questions, which ordinarily brief straightforward single word answers, so what you state does make a difference.

We all have been the one awkwardly posing inquiries of the individual we need to dazzle or interface with, just to end up running the conversation into a block divider. These kinds of questions limited down the potential reactions to a form of either yes or no. When you ask shut ended inquiries, you lead your conversation partner down a way that seriously restricts open doors for profundity and connection.

Things being what they are, in what ways are shut ended questions a piece of those conversations? How would we be able to liberate ourselves from this restricted method of talking?

Learning how to ask open-ended questions is important for effective communication in a relationship. There is an extremely basic methodology in how you talk with your loved ones that can upgrade your capacity to make better conversations—especially with your partner—and that is to ask open-ended inquiries. Open-ended questions originate from Miller and Rollnick's Motivational Interviewing, which is a generally acknowledged type of exchange that upgrades the member's inspiration to acknowledge the change. But open-ended questions are not just useful for treatment; they are likewise key to encouraging connecting with conversations in our regular day to day existence.

To more readily upgrade the open door for more profound, more extravagant conversation, as per

Miller and Rollnick, you need to chip away at your expressing of questions. Open-ended implies that the questions can't be properly replied with a basic "yes" or "no." Open-ended questions don't start with "do" or "did," which by and large brief a basic answer; open-ended kinds of questions, for the most part, start with these words: How did you, in what ways, outline for me, what's it like and so on.

If you have a high school student, imagine asking them this question by the day's end: "Did you have a decent day today?" Do you imagine that will incite an exciting conversation where your adolescent opens up to you pretty much the entirety of their deepest desires? Obviously it won't. Rather, you could attempt: "In what ways did you feel achieved today?"

Asking open-ended questions empowers the individual you're chatting with to think basically and along these lines to be all the more captivating, because open-ended questions permit the respondent, not the asker, to control the reaction.

Have a go at perusing the second section of this article once more, and notice how the passage totally contained open-ended questions that require significantly more basic ideas than the questions in the primary section. You are welcome to self-reflect and to jump into engaging answers that are ready for follow-up questions. In utilizing more open-ended questions in conversation, you welcome people to talk with you instead of talk to you. That is the formula for better conversations.

When it arrives at romantic relationships, asking open-ended inquiries is especially important, and The Gottman Institute's strategies urge couples to ask open-ended inquiries of one another all the time to extend their closeness. How about we envision those moments in a romantic relationship where the connection is difficult, where being busy is the norm, yet you long for a rich conversation with your partner like you used to have.

You go to your partner and ask, "Do you feel content with our relationship at the present time?" How can somebody start to address this inquiry when it may appear to be so reductive? We should revamp this inquiry to be more open-ended and perceive how it brings out conversation: "In what ways do you feel content with our relationship?" This open-ended model gives a considerably more useful setting to all the more likely know what is working out positively in the relationship.

Which carries us to this: better conversation is more helpless and more private conversation. It is exceptionally difficult to share your musings and emotions by responding to shut ended questions, but with open-ended questions, the entryway for more profound connectedness is flung all the way open. Without a doubt, you can't compel somebody to be open and genuine and share their more profound selves, but you can make a climate that welcomes further connection.

Open-ended questions expect us to be occupied with what we are stating. Also, when we are occupied with what we are stating, we make better and more important conversation.

If you feel like you just never relate with one another and things have been like this for some time, you may require a tad of outside help to kick things kick-off again.

It's in circumstances like this that directing can be extremely helpful. Your instructor will offer you both the chance to communicate and help you consider approaches to reconnect. They can help you talk about how you got to this point in any case and to investigate any issues that may have contributed.

9

WHEN YOU LISTEN, REALLY LISTEN

Communication is a two-way process consisting of conveying and getting the message. Therefore, a compelling communication in a relationship doesn't just incorporate the manner in which you talk to your partner, but how you listen all the time.

The capacity to listen to your partner well, especially when something is troubling them, is one of the most important relationship qualities you can have. Doing this makes your partner feel special and loved while additionally furnishing them with the knowledge that they have a sheltered spot to go to whenever they have to talk or feel that something isn't right. It can now and again be exceptionally difficult to listen to your partner without responding in an argumentative manner especially if it appears that they are scrutinizing you. It takes a ton of development to fight the temptation to safeguard yourself even with such s especially when you can't help contradicting what is being said or feel unjustifiably judged.

The aptitude of listening is especially important for men to ace. This is because women esteem a man who can listen to them exceptionally as in doing so they are satisfying one of the most important things women search for in a relationship. All the time women use talking as a method of working through their problems or different sorts of emotional stress while men then again want to take care of their problems inside and are more inclined to quietness while they make sense of things for themselves. Where women are concerned it is frequently the situation that you don't have to give them any answers or guidance, it is sufficient to be happy to listen mindfully to her as she works through her own procedure and discovers her own serene resolution.

For men, it involves expanding your restraint and to likewise set aside the effort to understand the other gender only somewhat better. By basically knowing how to listen accurately you can maintain a strategic distance from a lot of pointless arguments in a relationship. For women it is important not to anticipate that a man should consequently know this about you, rather you should assume liability for instructing him in what you need and trust that he thinks enough about the relationship to need to do what will make you cheerful and fulfill your essential needs.

Many people are acceptable in talking, especially when they're angry at someone. They even practice the lines that they are going to state, for the most part frightful words, so they feel better a while later. The problem is that it doesn't cause you to feel great. It just scars your relationship and that makes more problems later on. You need to understand that listening, and it's not talking, is the most important piece of communication.

HOW YOU CAN DEVELOP YOUR LISTENING SKILL AS A COUPLE

Listening to your spouse is by a wide margin, one of the most overlooked abilities in having a decent relationship. Many people are simply excessively occupied with different things that aren't generally part of the issue, or problem, that couples have. This is the motivation behind why this aptitude is created in marriage mentoring programs.

Recalling these things will help you build up your listening ability:

One of the things you should know is that agreeing or obeying isn't equivalent to listening. Have you at any point said "Listen to me!" to your partner, in marriage mentoring or a typical day at home, but what you truly implied is this - "You need to concur with me!"? Continuously recall that listening is, essentially, simply hearing and understanding what you two are attempting to state to one another, nothing else.

Also, until someone listens and understands, it's difficult to determine an issue. An issue that continues returning over and over is because of the way that no one listens in the relationship. One would state it's the other's shortcoming, and the other will do likewise - it is a ceaseless cycle. In settling an issue, both of you need to listen cautiously to what each is attempting to state.

To develop your listening skills, you should also understand that pain or fear results in outrage. Marriage mentoring programs state that when listening to your partner, remember that outrage is the consequence of pain or fear. Before being guarded and returning at your partner with outrage, know why your partner is harmed or frightened. Thus, you can have more sympathy in listening.

Between understanding couples, everyone accepts that their own suppositions and feelings are correct. You argue with your partner because you trust you are correct and the other isn't right. The other individual does likewise which never settles the issue if you don't listen. Listening helps you understand the truth of the conclusions and feelings of your partner. Allow your partner to clarify what they accept occurred.

WHY (AND HOW) TO BE A BETTER LISTENER IN YOUR RELATIONSHIP

Feelings of closeness and intimacy can get a relationship through difficult situations and help couples flourish when the relationship is acceptable.

One approach to fabricate closeness in your relationship is by imparting your considerations and feelings to one another and afterward reacting to those revelations such that causes you both to feel great. In relationships research, they call this being "receptive to your partner's needs." Being a responsive partner, and feeling like your partner is receptive to you, is truly at the center of good communication and closeness. When you feel like your partner truly gets you, you feel like nothing else matters.

Now the question is how would you be able to fabricate closeness intimacy with your partner? The initial step is being happy to reveal your musings and feelings to your partner. These exposures shouldn't be about your relationship (in spite of the fact that they can be). It's more about keeping you and your partner in a state of harmony by sharing the considerations that experience your psyche for the duration of the day. You may feel that the senseless web image you saw online does not merit mentioning, but if you set aside the effort to impart it to your partner, you are making a connection that integrates both of you. If you try not to enlighten your partner concerning your day, great and awful, of all shapes and sizes, you and your partner will start to carry on with discrete lives and this will raise separation instead of closeness.

Also, it is similarly as important that you ensure you are open to listening when your partner wants to impart their considerations and feelings to you. Try not to moan or take a gander at your telephone or state you don't have time. Rather, empower their exposures as an approach to support your partner and draw nearer to them. Their revelations may be something little and senseless to you, but it may be extremely significant to them.

You presumably don't have unlimited hours to sit and talk about your days and there might be times when you feel too occupied to even think about taking a couple of seconds for an inactive visit. But it's likely the most important to set aside some effort to do this when life is disrupting the general flow. If you just make some little memories together, that is even more motivation to manufacture closeness whenever and any place you can.

Preferably, this occurs face to face, but if you go through a large portion of your day separated, you can fabricate closeness for the duration of the day by sharing your musings and feelings via telephone, text, email, or online talk. See a news story that made you think? Send it to your partner and disclose to them why you enjoyed (or didn't care for) it. Hear a melody you loved on the radio on your approach to work? Email a connection of it to your partner when you have a moment and solicit what they think from it. Have a disappointing conversation with your chief? Venture outside for a moment and call your partner to vent.

The second means to building closeness is to be a

responsive listener when your partner reveals to you their considerations and feelings. What precisely does it intend to be a responsive listener? Some portion of it is that entire "don't moan and state you don't have time" piece. Express enthusiasm for your partner and be locked in. Set your telephone aside and show you are genuinely listening. At that point be understanding, validating, and mindful.

The first is being understanding. The objective is extremely about looking for understanding. You have to ensure you understand what your partner is attempting to state.

How to do it: Clarify what your partner is stating by asking them what they said or rehashing back to your partner what you think they said. You can do this with expressions, for example, "So what you are stating is...,`` " Would I be able to ensure I understand?" and "Would you be able to state that once more?"

Another way is to validate your partner's viewpoint. The objective here is extremely about ensuring your partner feels that you get what they are stating as well as why they are stating it. You have to ensure your partner knows that you truly get what their identity is and why they figure the manner in which they do and that you respect and value them.

How to do it: Let your partner know that you "get" them with phrases like "I can perceive any reason why that would be important to you," "I understand why you did that," "I can perceive any reason why you'd be extremely cheerful about that," "That more likely than not made you truly [insert emotion]." You can likewise communicate agreement with expressions, for example, "I'd feel that way as well" or "I'd do something very similar."

Being mindful is also another way to be a better listener. The goal here is is tied in with telling your partner they are loved and supported and that you are there for them.

How to do it: Be affectionate in your behavior and words (kiss, embrace, say "I love you"). Tell your partner you are in it together. "This issue to me as well," "This is important for the two of us," "We'll make sense of it together." If your partner is talking about something negative, express support ("I'm here for you," "Let me know how I can help"). If your partner is talking about something positive, express excitement and encouragement ("That's incredible! We should celebrate!").

TOP LISTENING ABILITIES TO BETTER YOUR RELATIONSHIP

Opening your heart to your spouse and sustaining theirs requires listening great. With so many different issues, commitments, gadgets, and people pulling at us from each course, it very well may be difficult to back off and genuinely listen to each other. Listening can be wonderful, but sometimes it's out and out hard. Sometimes, you should block out and lose yourself in your preferred pastime rather—or jump into the rundown of to-do things you despite everything need to check off before the day is finished.

But to have a sound, flourishing marriage, it's basic to really listen to your spouse with compassion and liberality. Today, we're sharing five different ways you can be a decent listener for your spouse

The first is to listen with empathy. When you practice sympathy, you're imagining your spouse's perspective and seeing things through their eyes. Regardless of whether you're attempting to determine a conflict or essentially listening to your spouse talk about their day, it's gainful to both of you to listen with sympathy when your spouse addresses you. For you, it gives you a window into their reality and their viewpoint. For your spouse, knowing that you're listening from an empathic vantage point helps them feel secure.

Possibly your spouse needs to vent about work, and typically, you block out when they begin talking about their intense day or their difficult undertaking. Rather than turning your psyche off while they talk, attempt to see the occasions of the day through their eyes, and with regards to your life. Have you been managing problems at home, as monetary issues, issues with the children, or dealing with a weak parent? Contextualizing your entire life alongside what's going on at your spouse's activity will help you understand the degree of heap they're managing.

Another listening ability is to listen for emotion. When your spouse needs to talk to you about something—especially if it's something hard—it's anything but difficult to get wrapped up and diverted by your own emotions on the subject. All things considered, you may react to your spouse in an absolutely unseemly manner in your endeavor to mitigate the difficult emotions that surface for you. Rather, pause for a moment to listen for what your spouse may be feeling. This sort of deliberate listening goes connected at the hip with sympathy.

When you've identified what your spouse is

feeling—regardless of whether it's annoyance, bitterness, disappointment, nervousness, or excitement—you can change your reactions dependent on their emotional state. It gives you an additional opportunity to take a look at yourself before you state or accomplish something that may worsen the emotional state they're in. When our emotions go into a spiral, it very well may be difficult to keep communication sound.

Listening without bias is another ability that will make you better understand your partner well. You've both heard your thoughts, and it's difficult to release those sentiments for basically listening to each other. Listening without predisposition is helpful when you have inverse positions on specific issues, or when you're secured an impasse during a fight. Put your sentiments in a safe spot for enough time to hear what your spouse is stating, at that point practice your sympathy abilities to attempt to understand why.

This doesn't mean you need to change your supposition to coordinate your spouse's. What it implies is that your spouse has the right to be heard, and you can't really hear if you're sifting all that they state through your own inclination.

Listening in a loving way goes a long way

towards better understanding your spouse as well. When you're speaking with your spouse, it very well may be helpful to utilize loving signals and non-verbal communication to tell them you care about what they need to state. It very well may be as basic as holding eye to eye connection and gesturing to avow what they're letting you know. You could likewise connect with touch them or clasp hands. Turn your body toward them, or even stop what you're doing and simply sit with them if that is what they need.

While you might have the option to continue on ahead and have a conversation simultaneously (and that can be alright sometimes), there will be times where you have to recently put everything down and center all your attention around your spouse. Mood killer the TV, put down your telephone or different gadgets, overlook the plan for the day for a brief period, and give your spouse loving attestation through eye to eye connection and to.

If you learn to listen generously, your spouse needs the gift of your time and attention. It's difficult to remove time from our bustling lives to liberally give our vitality to listening when we have such a great amount to do each day, but conveying openly is critical to a solid marriage. When you listen liberally, your spouse will feel secure in coming to you with their interests, expectations, and fears.

Convincingly, having the option to listen is probably the best expertise an individual can have in keeping up a decent relationship. When you listen to somebody and they truly feel like you have understood them then you will have a much simpler time getting them to listen to what you need to state when things are convoluted.

One issue that causes a lot of conflict in relationships is the absence of listening. If one individual in the relationship doesn't feel listened to appropriately, there can be some disappointment. Over the long haul, great communication will be vital to a sound enduring relationship so it's important to figure out how to listen to one another.

Be certain that while listening to things that you pose inquiries and rehash it with the goal that the other individual knows that you understand. Be certain that you don't sound excessively mocking while at the same time doing this else it can cause the other individual to feel like you are putting down their endeavors.

Ensure that your partner knows that you have the opportunity to listen to the person in question. This probably won't imply that you are doing so at the present time, but that the entryway is open for the person in question to communicate the things that should be said. Knowing one can be listened to can mean a great deal. This incorporates keeping numerous alternatives open for the individual to stand out enough to be noticed so you two can talk at a more profound level when required.

Every now and then remind your partner about the more profound and more important things that the person has communicated. This will show that you were listening as well as that you care enough to recall these things longer term. While you can't recall everything, give a valiant effort to attempt. The exertion will mean a lot.

ALWAYS RESPECT EACH OTHER

eople have many thoughts regarding what "respect" signifies. Sometimes, it is utilized to mean profound regard for somebody important or helpful to us. Different times, respect refers to regard towards a figure of power, similar to a parent, relative, instructor, chief or even a cop. In this unique situation, it is assumed that respect ought to be given to the people who have specific sorts of knowledge and force. And afterward different times, respect implies maintaining the essential right that each individual needs to settle on their own decisions and feel safe in their own day by day lives.

In this aspect of this guide, we're talking about respect with regards to dating. In a sound relationship, partners are approaches, which implies that neither one of the partners has "authority" over the other. Each partner is allowed to carry on with their own life, which can incorporate choosing to impart a few parts of their life to their partner. Respect additionally implies that, while we may not generally concur with our partner/s, we decide to confide in them and put confidence in their judgment. This trust can be worked after some time as your relationship advances and you study one another.

Respect is one of the most important parts of any relationship. It implies that you and your partner are rising to. Nobody remains over the other and everybody's voice is heard. When couples have respect, it lets loose them to be their own individual, having their own advantages, suppositions, and feelings unafraid of dismissal or retaliation from their partner. Respect is significant to a marriage's prosperity, as it frequently positions higher than love as far as what's generally important. This bodes well: After all, it's difficult to have one without the other. But respect can be difficult to quantify, especially as guardians when jobs change and dignity shift. All in all, what does respect really look like in a loving relationship? It fluctuates, obviously. But partners who respect each other make certain to do these 10 things.

Self-Respect - while it's important to respect your partner in a relationship, it's additionally extremely important to have respect for yourself, regardless of whether single or dating. Dignity is the way to building certainty and keeping up sound relationships with others for the duration of your life.

Things being what they are, what is self-respect? Confidence is an acknowledgment of yourself in general. It doesn't mean you believe you're great; actually, we as a whole merit respect despite the fact that we are NOT great. You have worth and worth because you're you. Dignity implies you hold yourself to your own guidelines, and you make an effort not to stress a lot over what others consider you. You deal with your body and psyche (or you're figuring out how!), regardless of whether that is through eating well nourishments, moving your body in manners that feel great to you, perusing and picking up, going to treatment, rehearsing your confidence or any number of things that respect what your identity is.

Why Respect Matters- respect is important in every single human relationship. If you can't respect somebody for what they've done, you can give them fundamental human respect or respect the job they play regardless of whether you don't respect the individual. Genuine respect, however, is especially important in love relationships. Because enduring love relationships help characterize who you are as an individual, it's urgent that the relationship is a solid one. When you and your partner respect one another, you make a sound relationship in which you can both develop and add individual quality all through your lifetime.

When you neglect to respect your partner, you keep yourself from receiving legit respect from them consequently. Your disappointment makes an environment where your partner can't be their best. Similarly as important, you put yourself in that equivalent environment, where love is more similar to an infection and a weight to both of you.

There is a lot of value in a respectful and loving relationship. Showing respect isn't just about maintaining a strategic distance from an awful relationship. It offers many positive advantages for you separately and for you and your partner as a couple. A respectful love relationship can help every one of you as people by giving you an emotionally protected space, building your fearlessness, allowing you opportunity and autonomy, fostering your self-awareness, increasing your inspiration to exceed expectations at what you do, Bringing you feelings of self-esteem and acknowledgment from another, helping you see the world in a positive light, the same sort of love can likewise do the accompanying for you as a couple, Improve communication inside the relationship, empower you to manage conflict in solid and beneficial manners, help you settle on better choices as a couple, let you appreciate each other's conversation more, Help you work out differences without cutting off the association and so on.

When you really love somebody, you need the best for them. If you need to put forth a strong effort, it makes sense that you need to give them your most extreme respect. How would you do that? You do it by the manner in which you consider them, communicate, and act toward them.

Another key is one that we frequently underestimate: stand by to get into a relationship until you meet somebody that you respect. When we face strain to be in a relationship from companions, the media, or even from inside ourselves, it tends to be anything but difficult to begin a relationship with somebody that we don't generally love or respect. Sometimes these relationships can turn out to be, but it bodes well to remain single until the correct individual tags along.

SEE YOUR PARTNER AS DESERVING OF RESPECT

If you don't see anything to respect about your partner, why are you still with them? You most likely accept there's something splendid about them. Maybe you simply haven't considered it much. If not, presently an extraordinary time. To start with, recollect that they merit fundamental human respect. At that point, consider the things you respect about them precisely. Consider their characteristics. Is it accurate to say that they are generally neighborly, funny, wise, or tranquil? What about their achievements? What have they done that intrigues you? What are they acceptable at? Is it accurate to say that they are an incredible craftsman, parent, businessman, or home decorator? Is it true that they are ready to do things others can't? You set up for approaching them with respect by concentrating on what makes your partner the remarkable mix of capacities, achievements, and individual characteristics that alone they are. It's important to recall that the things you consider frequently are the things that you're going to see the most.

If you're continually centered around the things that you don't respect about your partner, then it will be hard when you're constructing a wellbeing relationship that has respect in the establishment.

Being observant is a way to let your partner know that you respect him/her. You'll never know precisely how splendid your partner is if you don't observe what they do, how they carry on, and what they achieve. Construct your respect by seeing their victories. Notice which of their achievements makes them most joyful and know about their extraordinary attributes. Everybody has worth and something great in them. Some portion of achieving this is having constructed undivided attention abilities. When they talk, focus on pieces of information. If you're focusing, you'll see a greater amount of what makes them what their identity is. It's important in romantic relationships to deliberately search for the beneficial things in your partner.

Value Your Partner for Who They Are. Many people have that thought of what their ideal partner would resemble. This perfect picture doesn't help you construct respect for your partner. Put it in a safe spot, and recognize the truth about your partner. Rather than whining that they aren't what you might want them to be, commend them as they seem to be. This helps couples assemble solid relationships.

Another way to show your partner that he/she

deserves your respect is to constantly communicate Your respect. Your respect will affect your partner more when you communicate it well. Tell them what you respect about them. Show them how cheerful you are when they achieve something that intrigues you. You can communicate through words or looks of approval. Try not to stop complimenting them legitimately. Tell others how much you esteem their accomplishments and individual character. Sometimes, getting notification from their companions how you feel can be similarly as satisfying to your partner as hearing it from you and it can do wonders for building a romantic relationship.

Treat Your Partner as Inherently Valuable. Not A Means to an End. Your partner may help you from numerous points of view. They may urge you to give a valiant effort. They may help you in viable manners, as well, such as supporting you while you advance in your instruction or your vocation. Regardless of what they accomplish for you, however, don't dismiss their incentive in simply being what their identity is. Absolutely, you have to tell them you acknowledge what they accomplish for you. Go past that, however. When building positive relationships, let them know that in any event, when they aren't doing anything for you, you appreciate them in their own right.

Also, to respect your spouse, always choose to pick respectful actions. Recall when building well-being relationships, including a romantic relationship, each activity is a decision. Think before you act. Pick behaviors that show your respect. Give them the motivation to feel safe with you by not insulting them verbally or truly. Make time to be with them. Go along with them in commending their achievements. Be courteous to them.

Respect their decisions in any event, when they don't profit you. These things go far in making positive relationships.

It's anything but difficult to state that you have respect for somebody, but acting with respect can be somewhat trickier. That is why we need to talk about how you can show respect in your relationship. All things considered, because you don't genuinely hurt your partner or call them names, doesn't imply that you are approaching your partner with respect.

Here are six different ways that you can show your partner respect.

SIX WAYS TO SHOW RESPECT TO YOUR PARTNER

The first is to always exhibit trust. Trust is basic in any relationship, even non-romantic ones. But it implies significantly more than accepting that your partner won't undermine you, and feeling trust isn't close to as incredible as showing that you confide in your partner with your activities.

You can show trust by not messaging or calling your partner continually. Rather, text or call them once. Leave a message saying that you're considering them and that you plan to get notification from them soon. This shows you believe them to connect with you when they can, and that you know your partner values your endeavors.

This ought to abandon saying, but don't experience your partner's telephone or individual things without consent. If you have a bizarre feeling that they're attempting to conceal something from you, talk to them about it. There's no compelling reason to work up dramatization if there's nothing going on!

Secondly, be aware of how you communicate. Communication is one of the most important pieces of a relationship, and one of the hardest. That is because being open and legitimate with your partner implies being open and fair with yourself.

Try not to anticipate that your partner should be a brain reader. If you're disturbed, it's important to talk openly about what's irritating you. Try not to be accusatory. Use "I" statements, similar to "I feel truly disregarded and unimportant when you drop our arrangements finally," or "I feel irritated when you continue requesting that I hang out when you know I have to contemplate. I truly value it when others respect my time." Your emotions are consistently valid—don't feel awful for feeling what you feel.

Everybody differs sometimes, and that is absolutely alright. When you do, don't vanish or close down communication. At the very least, tell your partner that you're vexed and need some time to chill off and process your musings before you talk. Along these lines, they don't feel like you're vanishing on them or overlooking their feelings. Validate your partner's feelings by making statements like, "I understand why you feel that way," or "I hear what you're stating."

Communication goes amazing, however. You can tell your partner that you care by wearing the cologne they like, imparting a playlist to them, or bringing them blossoms.

Be dependable and responsible. A tremendous piece of a relationship is trust, but how would you be able to believe somebody if they're continually dropping plans or, far more atrocious, lying?

When you make arrangements, finish. Try not to express yes to a supper you don't know you'll have the option to go to. Rather, be responsible. Keep a schedule and check it when you and your partner are making arrangements. Try not to state you'll call and afterward don't. Rather, set an update on your telephone. Being trustworthy respects your partner's time and emotional vitality. All things considered, it very well may be stressful to have your arrangements change continually.

Obviously there will be times when you must choose the option to drop—there's a family crisis, you're wiped out, you overlooked a major test that you need to read for. You shouldn't feel liable (or be caused to feel blameworthy!) about these conditions. But it can help a great deal if you show you're mindful of the impact that those activities (regardless of whether they're inside your control or not) have on your partner. Apologize, offer to reschedule, and ensure you check in with them when you're free.

The third of all is to encourage time apart. When you're in a new relationship, you might be eager to the point that you need to invest all your energy with your partner. That is absolutely ordinary. But it tends to be barely noticeable in the other important relationships in your life, as with your loved ones. No single individual—regardless of how wonderful they are—can deal with all your social and emotional needs. Also, everybody needs a break from their significant other occasionally. Investing energy alone or with others implies that both of you can keep on developing as people. You can both carry new thoughts and exercises to your relationship, keeping it energizing and locks in. It likewise allows you both to talk about your relationship with your loved ones. Who wouldn't like to boast somewhat about their new love?

Another way is to always value your differences. Try not to condemn your partner for their thoughts or interests. You can differ with somebody and still respect their feelings. Some portion of what makes relationships magnificent is the differences! Your partner can help you see the world from another point of view, regardless of whether you don't conclusively adjust your perspective. You can show your partner you welcome them by heading off to their ball game or craftsmanship show, regardless of whether you could never go to a baseball arena or workmanship display in any case.

Acknowledge your partner's limits, in any event, when they're different from yours. If your partner wouldn't like to kiss in broad daylight, or engage in sexual relations, or lie to their folks, don't pressure them. This is coercive and possibly injurious.

Become more acquainted with yourself. In a relationship, you're not simply becoming more acquainted with someone else. You're becoming acquainted with yourself better. Being in a relationship can help you make sense of what you need and need from the people you're close with. What are you ready to settle on? Which characteristics complement your own? What are your basic beliefs that you can't settle on? Perhaps you couldn't care less that your partner isn't into R&B music the manner in which you are, but you can't stand that they're mean to your feline. Become more acquainted with yourself as an individual and as a partner. Knowing yourself helps you communicate better, and your partner will welcome that.

Knowing your own limits makes it much simpler to know when those limits have been crossed, and when you should cut off an association.

Showing respect may sound entangled, but it's

truly not. Everything comes down to listening to your partner and being caring for them.

WHAT IF YOUR RELATIONSHIP ISN'T LOVING OR RESPECTFUL?

If you're reading this and feeling that your romantic relationship is bound because it's missing love and respect, don't surrender. It's important to understand that there are many tips for building sound relationships that you can follow to change that. Here are a couple of amazing ways can assemble solid relationship aptitudes:

Create communication abilities. When you don't have the foggiest idea how to communicate inside a romantic relationship in a loving and respectful manner, you may discover endeavors you make in different regions won't make any difference. Work on building up your relationship with respect to communication until you're ready to feel more good doing it in any event, when it's a difficult conversation to have.

Practice undivided attention. When you have constructed undivided attention abilities, your partner may feel that you are showing them respect and love by intentionally focusing on them. This can help you fabricate a solid connection and romantic relationship.

Watch your non-verbal communication. You may feel that you're being respectful, but your non-verbal communication might be sending a different message. When you're in a romantic relationship, there are more employments of non-verbal communication that you can put to use too. Ensure you are utilizing your non-verbal communication to communicate love and respect.

Assemble your emotional insight. Emotional knowledge is your capacity to know about your emotions and have the option to deal with them in a solid manner. Improving here can help your mental wellbeing and help you in all aspects of your life.

Romantic relationships aren't in every case simple. Remember that building a long haul, sound relationship takes work. Regardless of whether you feel like your relationship had an incredible beginning, you may end up battling in the end. But by following tips for building a wellbeing relationship, you can turn it around.

If you need to have a passionate, lasting and successful relationship, at that point you need to begin with a gauge of shared respect. You need to ensure that you consider you to be your partner as a group and that you're kind, fair, and compassionate however much as could be expected. However, no one's ideal, and you must be set up to apologize truly when you have committed an error. If both you and your partner are eager to invest the exertion you can have a satisfying and respectful relationship.

11

OWN UP TO YOUR MISTAKES – TAKE FULL RESPONSIBILITY

Assuming ownership and responsibility for your deeds is an important part of sound relationships. Doing so is an engaging update that you have authority over the role you play in your relationship. Assuming responsibility creates trust and steadfastness between couples. When you take responsibility for your behaviors, you show your partner your eagerness to be completely forthright and defenseless, which in turn urges your partner to be open and credible with you.

Everybody makes mistakes. However, owning up to those mistakes might be more difficult for certain people. It might appear to be simpler to excuse your behavior as opposed to going up against reality and owning up to your mistakes. Dodging reality may put a strain on your relationship with somebody and it might be the reason for superfluous stress and concern. So when is it the opportune time to concede that you're off-base and what are the advantages to doing as such?

All through your marriage, you will commit errors. Albeit little mistakes won't at first hurt your marriage, if you don't acknowledge your mistakes, or you become cautious or justify your mistakes, those behaviors will make antagonism and an absence of trust among you and your spouse.

It doesn't have any effect if you've committed an insignificant error or a genuine misstep; you have to take ownership of the mix-up, admit to it, apologize for it, fix it, and not rehash it.

WHAT TAKING RESPONSIBILITY LOOKS LIKE

It is important to recognize assuming and diverting liability for both you and your partner. Know about protective reactions which may incorporate "quit being so delicate" or "I didn't know that you thought about that" or "you should've said something." It's not just important for you to assume liability. It's something that is important that your partner learns and does so as to have a sound relationship.

For you, assuming liability looks like rehearsing mindfulness. Another way is having the option to apologize and acknowledge that what you do influences your partner. For your partner, assuming liability looks like having open communication with you about their feelings and being eager to concede they can develop from the hard pieces of the relationship. Your partner figures out how to assume liability when they own their behaviors and consider themselves responsible for their activities.

The most serious issue is how it influences the individual who faults. Accusation influences people from various perspectives. Exploration shows that people who accuse others lose status, learn less, and perform more terribly comparative with others. Specifically... Blame makes inaction. When somebody faults, maybe they're giving over control of the circumstance. "I can't change until you do," is the certain message. The solution is in their partner's hands.

Blame isolates people from your qualities, convictions, and commitment. If the problem has a place with another person, at that point you have the motivation to delve in your heels. You pass up on a chance to develop, to extend, to challenge yourself. You may botch an opportunity to change the manner in which you think or act, or an opportunity to be profoundly legit: by sharing your fear, or disappointment, or bitterness in a sincere way.

Blames keep down genuine change. Blame feels worldwide and progressing. If you consider your to be as indifferent, you don't see the little moments of caring she offers. If you consider him to be indifferent, you don't see little offers of affection and respect. If you consider yours to be as languid, you don't see their endeavors – however irregular – to carry out the responsibility well. What's more, if you don't see the mindful, the respect, and the endeavors, you can't acknowledge them. Also, without acknowledgment, they start to blur.

TOLERATING MISPLACED BLAME

There is a critical difference between assuming liability and tolerating lost fault. Assuming liability is failing to accept fault for things you didn't do. For instance, when your partner reveals to you that something is your shortcoming, you don't consequently assume liability for whatever botch it was. It's basic in undesirable relationships, especially mutually dependent ones, for one individual (the manipulator) to state, "it's all your deficiency" and for his/her partner to state "it's all my issue." Many times, people may assume liability for things that are not their issue, and they may even do as such without intentionally acknowledging it. Rationalizing your partner's behavior or yourself is undesirable and may prompt these unfortunate behaviors being overlooked or acknowledged.

THE IMPORTANCE OF OWNING UP TO YOUR MISTAKES

Regardless of how difficult it is to counter the components of our personality safeguard framework, the errand isn't entirely inconceivable. Each man who wishes to accept the job of manhood must put forth the attempt. In doing as such, you will find that endeavoring to assume liability for your life and ownership of your mistakes is extraordinarily beneficial for many reasons.

One is that it permits you to settle on better choices. Self-justifications twist reality. The more you use them, the more you make an imaginary world for yourself. This prompts a diminished capacity to use sound judgment, as the information you're utilizing to do so is distorted. This can keep you from the people and interests that could have been beneficial for you – if just you had the option to recognize the truth about them obviously.

Most perilously, one self-justification brings forth another, setting off a huge impact that sends you increasingly more of it. When you justify a particular decision you made, you go deeper into it and make similar choices in the future, even when you doubt if it was the correct decision, you'll settle on that choice that delves you much further into it and that's how the cycle goes. For instance, if you hit a child at school, you'll at that point feel some discord in the fallout for hurting somebody (nobody likes to consider themselves savage), so you'll justify that choice by saying the child is an irritating crybaby who merited it. The more you harp on those justifi-cations, the more persuaded of them you'll become, and the more you'll feel like harassing him once more.

Another thing to gain is that it shields little prob-lems from transforming into large ones. Identified with the point above, if you can own up to a misstep when you make it and give a valiant effort to address it or make it right, you can keep it from transforming into a gigantic problem that will be difficult to comprehend. A snowballed misstep may destroy different parts of your relationships and vocation before you can get yourself free from it.

You also stand to gain from your mistakes if you own up to them. You can't gain from your mistakes if you can't acknowledge you've made them! What's more, if you don't gain from your mistakes, you're bound to rehash them. That is a formula for rapidly going no place in life.

If you take responsibility for your mistakes, it makes people respect you as well. We frequently conceal our mistakes from others because we stress they will consider less of us once they've seen that we've wrecked. But, honestly acknowledging your mistakes, saying 'sorry' for them, and afterward truly attempting to make things right quite often has the contrary impact– people respect you for it. There may in any case be outcomes, obviously, but people will value your genuineness. If they utilize your admission as an approach to deprecate and utilize you, those are most likely not the sort of people you need to work/live with at any rate. It's really when you conceal your mistakes, and they're discovered in any case, that people lose their respect and their trust in you.

Another advantage of owning up to your mistake

is that it reinforces relationships. Self-justification is a chilly, hard relationship executioner, as it makes us construct an instance of absolute fault against the other individual when things are going ineffectively between you.

There are two different ways to clarify mistakes: the individual did what they did because of the circumstance, or, because of what their identity is. We utilize the previous clarification with ourselves — "I overlooked her birthday because I have such a great amount at the forefront of my thoughts at this moment." We will in general utilize the second clarification on others — "She overlooked my birthday because she's so conceited." We don't evaluate their behavior, but their character – they don't do terrible stuff, they are awful. This sort of cover judgment is known as a worldwide mark. The individual is moronic, insane, futile, childish, juvenile, obnoxious, detestable, apathetic, and so on. They're a bombed human being.

Owning up to our mistakes permits us to assume liability for our lives. If we can't precisely see what our identity is, how we carry on (and how others act towards us), and how our behavior influences others and our own lives, life will consistently feel like something that is transpiring, instead of something we are in charge of

HOW TO OWN UP TO YOUR PARTNER

Envision this situation: "Why'd you put mustard all over my fries?" Jack inquires. At that point Jill answers, "Well, you should've disclosed to me you don't care for mustard!"

This is a case of how in many cases people redirect ownership of their behaviors and refuse to accept responsibility for the issues at hand. Is Jack answerable for his now mustard-secured fries, or ought to Jill have assumed liability for her behavior? Assuming liability in your relationship is the acknowledgment and ownership of each activity and word you state and do.

Assuming liability isn't only an uneven practice. The accompanying approaches to utilize the engaging move of making duty are important for both you and your partner to utilize and rehearse in your relationship.

Being honest also helps you to accept your faults in your relationships too. "You need to love yourself before you love others" is a flexible expression that has various implications when applied to relationships. It can make an interpretation of "You must be straightforward with yourself before you can be straightforward with others." Being straightforward with yourself starts with a sound feeling of mindfulness. What's more, acting naturally mindful methods you acknowledge that what you state and do impacts your partner.

Alluding back to the mustard circumstance, envision you're Jill. A sound reaction is to take ownership of her activities and react with something like, "Gracious, I'm grieved! I ought to have asked you before I included mustard. I didn't understand you didn't care for mustard, and this is my misstep."

Follow up on Situations, Don't React. When people are considered responsible for their behaviors, they regularly become guarded. Getting cautious is a response. When you follow up on a circumstance, you can react with lucidity and mindfulness. You can work on following up on circumstances as opposed to responding by taking full breaths or tallying to ten. It additionally helps to take a second and take a gander at the circumstance from your partner's point of view. It may very well be difficult to think from the other point of view, especially without giving it much thought. By being straightforward with yourself and your partner, you can viably react by assuming liability.

For instance: Jill is responding to Jack being disturbed as opposed to following up on her need to assume liability. Acting as opposed to responding permits you to plainly characterize a mindful and genuine response to undesirable behavior.

Be Eager to Forgive Your Partner and Yourself. Everybody commits errors and forgiving yourself or your partner is important for moving past difficulties and making your relationship more grounded. When you see accepting obligation regarding your mistakes as a chance to learn, your relationship can turn into a spot that cultivates and praises growth. Absolution manufactures trust and responsibility in your relationship, separates resentment, and stops the in no way enjoyable "habitual pettiness."

Assuming liability for your behaviors in your relationship requires genuine and open communication and a readiness to address unfortunate reasons with your partner. They're not in every case simple conversations to have, but you'll see that doing so assembles trust inside your relationship after some time and is an enabling method to learn and develop.

THE POWER OF AN APOLOGY: WHY LOVE MEANS SAYING "I'M SORRY"

Why Apologize? There are many reasons why you should make an earnest expression of remorse when you've harmed somebody superfluously or have committed an error.

Initially, a conciliatory sentiment opens an exchange among yourself and the other individual. Your ability to concede your slip-up can give the other individual the open door he needs to communicate with you, and begin managing his feelings.

When you apologize, you likewise acknowledge that you are occupied with unsatisfactory behavior. This helps you revamp trust and restore your relationship with the other individual. It additionally allows you to examine what is and isn't worthy.

What's more, when you concede that the circumstance was your deficiency, you reestablish respect to the individual you hurt. This can start the recuperating procedure, and it can guarantee that she doesn't unreasonably reprimand herself for what occurred.

Last, a true statement of regret shows that you're assuming liability for your activities. This can reinforce your fearlessness, confidence, and notoriety. You're additionally prone to feel a liberating sensation when you confess about your activities, and it's perhaps the most ideal approach to reestablish your trustworthiness according to other people.

What are the outcomes if you don't apologize when you've made a mistake?

Initially, you will harm your relationships with partners, customers, companions, or family. It can hurt your notoriety, limit your profession openings, and lower your viability – and, others might not have any desire to work with you.

It likewise contrarily influences your group when you don't apologize. Nobody wants to work for a supervisor who can't own up to his mistakes, and who doesn't apologize for them. The enmity, pressure, and pain that accompanies this can make a harmful workplace.

Have you ever thought why apologies are difficult? With all these antagonistic results, why do a few people despite everything won't apologize?

To start with, expressions of remorse take mental fortitude. When you concede that you weren't right, it places you in a weak position, which can open you up to or fault. A few people battle to show this fearlessness.

On the other hand, you might be so loaded with disgrace and embarrassment over your activities that you can't force yourself to confront the other individual.

Or then again, you might be following the guidance "never apologize, never clarify." It's up to you if you need to be this egotistical, but, if you do, don't hope to be seen as an astute or a motivating head.

Saying 'sorry' is essential, since it helps to smooth any conflict and restore a profound connection with the partner. If you ace the specialty of saying 'sorry' it will help you diminish relationship stress and to proceed onward from conflicts and pressures. There are many demonstrated advantages of saying 'sorry'

- When you state that you are grieved, it reestablishes the poise of the hurt individual and causes them to feel better. The offended party, who receives the expression of remorse, creates compassion towards the wrongdoer, which at that point changes their feeling of hurt into pardoning.
- A conciliatory sentiment may reestablish trust and understanding to a relationship because it contributes to a feeling of security and causes both the receiver and the provider to feel good and respected.

Saying 'sorry' in this way helps you and your loved one remain emotionally associated, and reinforces the bond between both of you.

- When you make an earnest expression of remorse, and this trust and understanding gets reestablished, an individual can begin to see you in a different light. They will have a more noteworthy inclination to disregard your defects and feature your ethics.

- A powerful expression of remorse doesn't only mend the injury for the other individual, but also disintegrate your blame as well. By doing so, you eventually build up a feeling of self-respect and the ability to move on afterwards. Furthermore, It fills in as a hindrance, with the goal that you don't repeat similar mistakes.

Some accept that conceding you're off-base is an indication of shortcoming. As opposed to that conviction, I believe that owning your mistakes shows that you are sufficiently able to go up against reality paying little heed to the outcomes. Not acknowledging your mistakes implies that you are either inside or remotely accusing someone else. Accusing somebody who isn't to blame can harm the relationship you have with that individual. Subsequently, it's important to apologize when you have accomplished something incorrectly. Thus, you can proceed onward and gain from your slip-up.

12

LIVE YOUR OWN LIFE TOO

Having a specific measure of emotional dependency on your partner is normal. That is, by its tendency, scarcely broken. However, when it's unreasonable, it stops to be sound —not for you, your partner, nor the relationship by and large.

The writing on social dependency in grown-ups underscores that it's important your partner has the option to offer you emotional support when it's required. That, all things considered, is firmly associated with feeling substance, safe, and cheerful in any relationship—especially a submitted one. It's continually consoling to know that your significant difference has your back, that they'll be there for you even in circumstances where you two don't agree. Besides, their availability to validate your perspectives and behavior, to view them as bona fide and by and by important—and in spite of their point of view not continually concurring with yours—can support your certainty and confidence.

But once we substitute the word dependency for support, we're taking a look at something very different. Why? Just because, as that term is normally utilized in treatment, it suggests that we can't satisfactorily validate or alleviate ourselves, that we have to depend on our significant other to give us the consolation that we're adequate, and sufficiently important, to merit their unrestricted love.

In such a case, being unsure of our partner's approval or commitment to us, we wind up concentrating as much on our questions as we think about them. When we can't feel adequately sure about a relationship, our love for them is (unprepared) displaced by fear: Might they leave us? Reject us? Supplant us? Surrender us? What's more, the more we should depend on their consolation to feel esteemed, the more we'll stay dependent on them. What's more, in the long run, this can prompt the relationship's debasement.

The problem here is that it's difficult to love somebody—and let them be liberated to be what their identity is—when, unknowingly, we need them to help us conceal past weaknesses. These weaknesses start significantly less from our present-day partner as from our prior history, regularly because, while growing up, our folks couldn't cause us to feel safely appended to them.

Also, as much consolation as our partner might be eager to offer us, we'll continually be looking for additional. That is because if we were infrequently ready to experience our folks' unrestricted acknowledgment when we were kids, we'll have extraordinary difficulty disguising whatever consolation our partner would now be able to offer us. Without a doubt, at the time we might be mitigated, take it in, and be helped. However, except if we can somehow clutch their consolation, secure it from inside, and make it a characteristic piece of a presently patched up mental self-view, their endeavors for our sake won't last. Their soothing words will before long blur from awareness. And afterward we'll need—and may even demand—more, and that's only the tip of the iceberg, of the equivalent. Like an espresso mug with an opening in the base, however much is filled it, it will before long be vacant once more.

LIVING YOUR LIFE FOR YOURSELF

When you are approaching how to live for yourself, it implies that you have recently understood that you have been giving the vast majority of your time, ability, and vitality to other people and have put their needs before yours. Clearly, every now and then, we do that for our loved ones, but it happens once in a while that you commit your life to someone else or even an incredible reason, except if you are Nelson Mandela or Mahatma Gandhi.

I am happy to the point that you are asking this question, and it would appear that now you are going to assume liability for satisfying your own wants and needs. It doesn't make a difference at what age or phase of life you are in. It is sufficient that you have understood the need to remain consistent with yourself and make your life beneficial.

Living for Yourself Means Loving Yourself. Sometimes, you wrongly think that if you live for yourself, it is narrow-minded. It is seen that if you love yourself it is narrow-minded because this is what you were educated as a kid. In all actuality, there's no more prominent award in life other than to live for yourself and offer your novel abilities, qualities, and intelligence with the world. If you have a little confidence in your creation, you are a manifestation of love; God loves you, ensures you, so why not love God's creation with your own life and your motivation in life. Then again, characters like Nelson Mandela or Mahatma Gandhi were, indeed, the most narrow-minded people who loved themselves over and past anyone considers them. They loved themselves so much that they chose to carry on with life their way and leave their name alive in the entirety of mankind's history for eternity. Simply consider it.

Living For Yourself Means Confidence. So as to remain consistent with yourself and carry on with life your way, you'll need to have a degree of certainty to conquer all the snags and difficulties that tag along your way. You'll have to have faith in your hunch that you are correct and you can make it. With certainty about needing something so terrible, you can cause everybody to trust you know what you are doing. Is it accurate to say that you are prepared?

You need to quit thinking and start living. Sometimes, you think a great deal and are consistently in arrangement and arranging mode that you don't get the chance to practice and experience things that you have at the top of the priority list. I was one of these people. With no valid explanation, I felt that I am not prepared, or the time that I satisfy my dreams has not come at this point. I generally realized what to do when the time comes; I discovered euphoria in planning and in deduction, but that doesn't serve me anymore. Presently, I am additionally at a high point not to plan excessively and begin making a move regardless of whether they are not great. I am prepared to settle on choices quickly and without a great deal of reasoning. My new perspective about life is this: Living is encountering not considering the experience.

Three things will help you to begin once again and decide to carry on with life with reason: Take obligation regarding your own bliss and your own life. It requires some work, know precisely what makes you upbeat and begin encountering them individually, get free of your own self-constraining convictions because nobody is compelling you not to live for yourself

SIGNS YOU'RE TOO DEPENDENT ON YOUR PARTNER

Whenever you consider being in a relationship with somebody, you may consequently consider the love you have for the other individual and how much you rely upon them being in your life. But with this reliance accompanies indications of controlling behavior that you ought to consistently watch out for too.

While they may seem like two different things, being totally dependent on your partner and being constrained by your partner can frequently go connected at the hip. A controlling partner will frequently make you dependent to suit their needs: They'll get frantic if you spend time with companions, they don't do things you like to do, or they may even power you to cut binds with companions they don't care for.

It's important to recall that requiring an individual an excess of for the most part originates from fear, not love. When a partner makes their Significant other answerable for their own bliss, the need of having that validation nearly becomes like a dependence. They control their partner and it begins to turn into an emotional dependency because they fear losing their partner. While it will undoubtedly change over the span of a relationship, being horribly codependent can make you totally sacrifice your own character for your partner. Your self-esteem may even be dependent on the relationship without you in any event, acknowledging it. Perfect relationships are a decent equalization of dealing with the person just as making a relationship that is commonly fulfilling. If you're uncertain if your relationship is going a solid way or not, here are a few signs to watch to check whether you're in an emotionally dependent relationship.

One sign is that your happiness depends on your partner's mood. You attempt to ensure your partner is cheerful in any event, when it may make you miserable. It's OK to be thoughtful, but when you're possibly fulfilled when your partner is content, it might mean you're a piece excessively dependent. It's as yet important to be your own individual with your own brain, else, you'll be hopeless all the time because you're continually stressed about how your partner is feeling. Try not to let your partner's temperament assume control over yours.

When you don't care to spend time with your loved ones is also another sign. You deliberately abstain from making arrangements with your loved ones and like to invest energy just with your lover. If not this, you spend time with your precious ones just when your partner is occupied elsewhere. You are gradually putting some distance between your companions and in the end, demolishing your public activity.

When you also can't seem to do anything with your partner. This shows you are too dependent on your partner as well. You won't let your significant other do anything without you. You end up rationalizing not going to things because your partner can't go with you. You scarcely observe your companions any longer and when you do, it's never independent. It's critical to keep up your own character for your emotional wellbeing, and having the option to do things independently is a major piece of that.

When your arrangements are dependent on your partner, regardless of whether it is going for a film, shopping for food, or getting away, you have gotten dependent on your partner for each seemingly insignificant detail. You begin rationalizing the moment you are relied upon to accomplish something without anyone else and you probably won't have acknowledged but you battle to make regular choices without including your partner.

Constantly looking for validation is another pointer that you are too dependent on. Your relationship has become your lone source of satisfaction and you need steady consolation from your partner to remain glad. You search for your partner's validation to feel satisfied and fulfilled in life and your mindset relies upon how your partner is feeling.

When you give up your needs for your spouse is another pointer to the fact that you're overdependent. It's entirely expected to need to take into account your partner's needs sometimes, but you have to meet your own also. When everything you do is give and don't receive anything consequently, the relationship can get unfortunate and imbalanced. You may wind up detonating eventually, and you may feel void inside because you've overlooked yourself for such a long time.

When you feel jealous when your partner gives another person a few moments of attention. You get distraught when your partner talks to, invests energy with, or helps others, especially when it's a close friend or a relative. You come up with idiotic reasons for why your partner shouldn't talk to every individual. You need their attention to be completely on you consistently, regardless of whether you know it's stinging their different relationships. It's fine to need some attention and validation, but permit your partner to sustain different relationships as well. Else, they'll become angry and disappointed.

You've begun to lose your personality. This is another sign you should beware of, your whole spotlight has shifted on your relationship and your reality rotates around it. You have changed your day by day calendar and lifestyle according to your partner's preferences. Possibly, you used to take strolls or meet companions in your extra time, but now you just play computer games or gorge on web arrangement because this is what your partner appreciates. Keep in mind, it is a great idea to be interested and engage in your partner's pastimes and zones of intrigue but not to the degree that you begin losing your own character.

BECOMING EMOTIONALLY SELF-RELIANT

Generally, this manner of thinking begins in youth. We depend on our folks for our emotional needs — love, comfort, support, validation, and so forth. What's more, we don't regularly create emotional confidence aptitudes as children, because guardians (out of love for us) give a valiant effort to accommodate every one of these needs.

And afterward, we become grown-ups without having learned emotional independence. Thus we search for another person to fill our emotional needs. We search for the ideal partner, and will most likely experience a couple of separations, because, firstly, we're not emotionally independent, and as such, we do things that hurt our relationship, and also makes our partner behave in a similar way.If we're at any point hurt, we censor the other individual for hurting us. If they aren't there for us, we accuse them. If something terrible transpires, we become casualties, because you can't proceed onward with your life if somebody has planned something awful for you, isn't that so? However, there is a solution. There are approaches you can utilize to make you less Clingy In your relationship.

The first is to work on any trust issues you have. It can seem like an easy decision, but it's fantastically important to confide in your partner. If you don't confide in that person, at that point it will be difficult to let your partner have the space to be who the individual truly is. Not having trust in your significant other can cause the person in question to feel less sure about the relationship and lead to feelings of resentment. Trust is critical to keeping up a decent, long haul relationship that will satisfy both of you. Setting trust in your partner can mean anything from not continually asking where the person in question is during the day, to advising yourself that in any event, getting baffled with this new advance is useful for your relationship, in any event, when it doesn't appear as though it is.

Secondly, let people have their space. Love

doesn't mean you and your partner should be appended at the hip. For many couples, a lot of closeness can put a strain on the relationship. While sharing— contemplations, feelings, space, whatever — is certainly acceptable in any relationship, an excess of sharing can cause your significant other to feel caught. Nobody wants to choke in a relationship. It's ideal to give your partner the space the person in question needs. That way, your partner is more averse to connect your relationship with negative feelings, which makes the relationship more grounded over the long haul.

Develop trust in yourself. Self-assurance can go far in guaranteeing that you feel great in a relationship. People with more self-assurance are more averse to stick to others as a method of validating themselves. Think about rehearsing positive reasoning and self-esteem. If you respect and love yourself, it makes it that much simpler for others to do likewise.

To become emotionally self-dependent, you need to concentrate on yourself. Set aside some effort to truly fixate your musings on yourself. It's stunning how much we can find out about ourselves and our feelings if we simply set aside the effort to consider things alone. Set aside some effort to center your contemplations internally. Time alone can truly help you feel focused and rested, but it can likewise show your significant other that you're not dependent on the person in question for joy. Dependency can prompt one partner to feel more capable in the relationship than the other, which can prompt serious problems later on.

In this journey of being self-reliant emotionally, you have to know how to manage your nervousness. If you're inclined to nervousness or nerves, it very well may be anything but difficult to go to your partner as an approach to facilitate that distress. However, this can cause your partner to feel excessively liable for your bliss and can be an irregular method to manage your feelings. Rather, take a stab at transforming that tension into something positive and steady, for example, an everyday custom or movement. Essentially doing ongoing errands can ease on edge feelings and leave you with more positive vitality to place into the relationship. If you get yourself incessantly restless or with feelings that can't be managed effectively, address a specialist.

When one is in a codependent relationship, and depending intensely on the partner to satisfy their own bliss, they for the most part don't feel great about themselves. People in sound relationships find different outlets to satisfy them, regardless of whether it's their pastimes, their family, their activity, and so forth. But when your relationship doesn't include a sense of pride, it empowers awful behavior from your partner, and this could impact you to not feel great about yourself.

There are various approaches to mend from a codependent relationship. When you understand that you're in one, you can without much of a stretch find a way to beat it. It will require some investment and perhaps treatment, but the initial step is to acknowledge that you are surely codependent, and from that point, you can attempt to better yourself and your relationship.

Communication is the main driver behind humankind, after all, if we can't communicate information and insight, how can we keep moving forward? Look at all the impacts of contact, from the day we are birthed to when we pass; our minds are full of contact. Either communication is verbal or visual everywhere we look at people, houses, vehicles, and everything else you can see or hear, they're all transmitting their own meaning. If this is what contact can do to the senses on an ordinary daily basis, then the effect of interaction in relationships cannot be overstated.

Consider how you're building a relationship. You see somebody who's catching your eye; you go to talk to them. Now I assure you that fantasy gives you your early bonding, but it is by interacting together and knowing about one another that formal attachment will become a relationship. While dating, you share your thoughts, and yes, you chat a little more; given that what you know about one another isn't unnecessarily upsetting, then you embark into a much more steady relationship, you just might eventually wind up marrying. Without the effect of dialogue in relationships, a relationship could never be established or developed.

Relationship communication is critical. When spouses have difficulties in a relationship, communication will be the first thing that will stop. It's always better to be silent than to get angry. When redeveloping love and marital relationships, much like interaction is the first one to stop, now it requires to be the first to commence. This will demand both persons to let their things slide and to throw a lot of caution at the wind. Rejuvenation in a relationship can't start before you talk. Reach an agreement that you're going to talk about anything and everything, and that you're going to listen, really listen. That doesn't mean you're going to agree with anything, which is perfectly normal.

Nevertheless, if you do not accept, do not contend, but the two of you need to respectfully discuss the topic and come up with a solution collectively. This requires a lot of hard work, but in a really brief period, both of you will feel happier, personally, and as a couple.

Get in the routine of paying attention to whatever your partner is saying. Not any kind of hearing you do when you're out or fall asleep at the table eating, but a unique kind of communication. Have you ever noticed your friend make a remark to a friend or relative about something they would want or need to do? You might have heard your boyfriend or husband say to a friend that they'd love some kind of tool. For no excuse at all, make an extra effort to get something for him. You may have overheard your wife or girlfriend talk about a massage they'd probably try. Again, for no reason, show a surprise to her. This goes to show that your friend is really paying attention to things that are really important to you.

Many of the population have never known how to talk. Without this ability, a person is disabled in a romantic relationship. The partners can not achieve intimacy without being able to express themselves and listen to others. Through improving your interpersonal skills, you and your spouse will be able to build and sustain caring, meaningful relationships between people who value each other.

Married people who don't strive to interact actively will face challenges when it comes to closeness, confrontation, and interpersonal development. Comprehending the inner world of your partner and having them understand yours is central to a true connection. If you're struggling to communicate verbally that's changing your relationship, then over time, you'll find that you're growing apart.

The lack of relationship communication cannot be overlooked, particularly in circumstances where you feel like you can't communicate effectively with your partner.

Communication ties you together, links you to each other's lives, introduces you to who they are and what makes them click, gives you history, a present, and a future. If you don't have communication within a relationship, you have nothing to tie you together. If you have nothing to tie you together, you have no relationship.

Communication in your relationship is a no brainer. Ask each other what you did on the day you went, who you saw. Life would be pretty dull if you weren't able to tell your partner such. Let's go a bit further, think about your dreams and aspirations. If your marriage is going to grow, you have to be on the similar page and have a similar long-term vision to work to ensure stability and permanence in your relationship. And then, at the heart of things, you need to be willing to share feelings, emotions, needs, and desires, major issues. Your partner needs to understand how and when to support you, and to guarantee that your intimacy requirements are satisfied, as your best friend, they should be the first person that you turn to in times of need. There's no getting away from it, communication has a major impact on your relationships.

As a couple, always try to talk with each other. Irrespective of how well you love and know each other, you didn't interpret your spouse's mind. We need to talk effectively to avoid any misconceptions that can cause hurt, frustration, dissatisfaction, or uncertainty.

It takes multiple individuals to always have a relationship, and each has various communication styles and preferences. Couples need to learn to communicate that best serves their marriage. Sustainable styles of communication involve practice and dedication. Communication is never going to be flawless all the time.

When you talk to your partner, attempt to: put aside time to talk, consider what you need to state, be clear about what you need to communicate, make your message understood, so your partner hears it precisely and understands what you mean, talk about what is going on and how it influences you, talk about what you want, need and feel – use 'I' statements, for example, 'I need', 'I want' and 'I feel,' acknowledge duty regarding your own feelings, listen to your partner. Set aside your own contemplations until further notice and attempt to understand their aims, beliefs, needs and wants (this is called compassion), share positive feelings with your partner, for example, what you acknowledge and appreciate about them, and how important they are to you, know about your manner of speaking, arrange and recollect that you don't need to be correct always. If the issue you are having isn't unreasonably important, attempt to release the subject, or settle on a truce.

Be clear when speaking with your partner, so your message can be received and understood. Double-check your understanding of what your partner is stating.

Suppose you need to assemble a healthy relationship. In that case, it must be totally open and fair, you have to share your lives, which could feel somewhat meddlesome from the start, but your exertion will be more than rewarded by the nature of your relationship. One thing that I should mention and that it doesn't keep privileged insights! Not exclusively can your non-verbal communication part with you, but privileged insights have a method of being discovered, and that could decimate your relationship.

Indeed, even the most apparently perfect couples have their terrible days. You would prefer not to argue with your partner, but like it or not, that is what will occur. Presently here is the place communication can have a substantial effect on relationships. An issue comes up in your relationship; currently, you have two options, you can yell and shout at one another like a couple of children and accomplish nothing, or (and this is the place it gets radical) you can see that you have a problem, so both of your plunk down and attempt to figure out how to manage it.

When you manage issues, you are not hoping to score points, you are not going all out for a resolution that suits you best, and you are searching for a compromise that gives the best outcome for your relationship.

Not many individuals know this, but the chances of your partner being clairvoyant are actually very thin. If you need them to know something at that point, TELL them, don't feel that they should know consequently, or drop unimaginably obscure clues with the expectation that they will understand what you mean. Try not to be reluctant to state something; if it is certifiable and you say it respectfully, your partner should have no problem with it. The questions can begin if you don't mention anything, or if you trust that your partner will say something while they are sitting tight for you, or if you overlook something and expect it to disappear. If you have an issue or a need and you make no mention of it, at that point, it won't go; it will deteriorate and lead to resentment because your partner ought to have known.

The effect of communication on relationships is gigantic; if you don't communicate, you won't have a relationship. Communication can unite you, it can help your relationship develop, and your love grows. It doesn't take a lot to talk and to share your life, you can increase, and a lot of further understanding and connection with your spouse, in addition to it, makes life much more fascinating. If you need a loving, stable relationship.

REFERENCES

Bailey, Sandra (2009). "Couple Relationships: Communication and Conflict Resolution" (PDF). *MSU Extension*. **17**: 2. Archived from the original (PDF) on 2017-12-15. Retrieved 2016-12-05 – via George Mason University Libraries.

Nageshwar Rao, Rajendra P. Das, *Communication skills*, Himalaya Publishing House, 9789350516669, p. 48

Archived copy". Archived from the original on 2013-07-18. Retrieved 2012-09-29.

"Incorrect Link to Beyond Intractability Essay". Beyond Intractability. 2017-04-18. Retrieved 2017-05-01.

Chapman, Gary D.; Campbell, Ross (1997). *The 5 Love Languages of Children: The Secret to Loving*

Children Effectively. Chicago: Northfield Publishing. ISBN 9780802403476. OCLC 1020412967.

David Rainey (2008). *Faith Reads: A Selective Guide to Christian Nonfiction*. ABC-CLIO. p. 125. ISBN 978-1591588474.

Chapman and White, Northfield Press (2011), Appreciation at Work network[ISBN missing]

Chapman, Gary D.; Green, Jocelyn (2013). *The 5 Love Languages Military Edition: The Secret to Love That Lasts*. Chicago: Northfield Publishing. ISBN 9780802407696. OCLC 847246629.

"Important Components of Cross-Cultural Communication Essay". *Studymode.com*. Retrieved 2017-05-01.

Portable Document Format (PDF)". *Ijdesign.org*. Archived from the original on 2017-05-14. Retrieved 2017-05-01.

C.E. Shannon. "A Mathematical Theory of Communication" (PDF). *Math.harvard.edu*. Retrieved 2017-05-01.

"Types of Body Language". *Simplybodylanguage.com*. Retrieved 2016-02-08.Wazlawick, Paul (1970's) opus

(Burgoon, J., Guerrero, L., Floyd, K., (2010). Nonverbal Communication, Taylor & Francis. p. 3)

Martin-Rubió, Xavier (2018-09-30). *Contextual-*

ising English as a Lingua Franca: From Data to Insights. Cambridge Scholars Publishing. ISBN 978-1-5275-1696-0.

"communication". *The office of superintendent of Public Instruction.* Washington

Barkhuysen, P., Krahmer, E., Swerts, M., (2004) Audiovisual Perception of Communication Problems, ISCA Archive http://www.isca-speech.org/archive

Bretherton, I., (1992) The Origins of Attachment Theory: John Bowlby and Mary Ainsworth, Developmental Psychology, 28, 759-775

Mazza, J., Emotional Triggers, MABC, CPC

Bertram, M., (2004) How the Mind Explains Behavior: Folk Explanations, Meaning, and Social Interaction, MIT Press, ISBN 978-0-262-13445-3

"Listening". *2012books.lardbucket.org.* Retrieved 2017-05-01.

Lipthrott, D., What IS Relationship? What is Ethical Partnership?

Hearn, J., (2006) Interpersonal Deception Theory: Ten Lessons for Negotiators

Lenhart, A., Duggan, M., (2014) Couples, the Internet, and Social Media

Robbins, S., Judge, T., Millett, B., & Boyle, M.

(2011). Organisational Behaviour. 6th ed. Pearson, French's Forest, NSW pp. 315–317.

Baxter, L.A. (1982). Strategies for ending relationships: Two studies, *Western Journal of Speech Communication*, 46, 223–241.

Stephen M.R. Covey; Rebecca R. Merrill (2006). *The Speed of Trust: The One Thing that Changes Everything.* Simon & Schuster. p. 212. ISBN 978-1416542377.

Michael Olpin; Margie Hesson (2009). *Stress Management for Life* (2 ed.). Cengage Learning. p. 205. ISBN 978-0324599435.

Egbert, Nichole; Polk, Denise (23 Aug 2006). "Speaking the Language of Relational Maintenance: A Validity Test of Chapman's Five Love Languages". *Communication Research Reports.* **23** (1): 19–26. doi:10.1080/17464090500535822.

Feiler, Bruce (19 November 2011). "Can Gary Chapman Save Your Marriage?--This Life". *The New York Times.* Retrieved 1 April 2019.

Baxter, L.A. (1984). Trajectories of relationship disengagement. *Journal of Social and Personal Relationships*, 1, 29–48.

Davis, M.S. (1973). *Intimate relations.* New York: The Free Press.

Duck, S. (Ed.). (1982). *Personal relations 4:*

Dissolving personal relationships. New York: Academic Press.

Frankel, V. & Tien, E. (1993). *The heartbreak handbook*. New York: Fawcett/Columbine.

Guerrero, L.K., Andersen, P.A. & Afifi, W.A. (2007) *Close Encounters, communication in relationships*. Thousand Oaks, CA: Sage Publications.

Harvey, J.H. (1996). *Embracing their memory*. Boston: Allyn & Bacon.

Hill, T., Rubin, Z., Pepln, L.A. (1976). Breakups before marriage: The end of 103 affairs. *Journal of Social Issues*, 33, 197–198.

Johnson, M.P. (1982). Social and cognitive features of the dissolution of commitment to relationships. In S. Duck (Ed.), *Dissolving personal relationships* (pp. 51–73). New York: Academic Press.

Berscheid E (April 1999). "The greening of relationship science". *The American Psychologist*. 4. **54** (4): 260–6. doi:10.1037/0003-066X.54.4.260. PMID 10217995.

Acker M, Davis MH (1992). "Intimacy, Passion and Commitment in Adult Romantic Relationships: A Test of the Triangular Theory of Love". *Journal of Social and Personal Relationships*. **9** (1): 21–50. doi:10.1177/0265407592091002.:

Gibson LS (2015). "The Science of Romantic

Love: Distinct Evolutionary, Neural, and Hormonal Characteristics". *International Journal of Undergraduate Research and Creative Activities*. **7** (1): 1. doi:10.7710/2168-0620.1036.

Sternberg RJ (1986). "A triangular theory of love". *Psychological Review*. **93** (2): 119–135. doi:10.1037/0033-295x.93.2.119.

Hazan C, Shaver P (March 1987). "Romantic love conceptualized as an attachment process". *Journal of Personality and Social Psychology*. **52** (3): 511–24. doi:10.1037/0022-3514.52.3.511. PMID 3572722.

Vangelisti AL. "Interpersonal processes in romantic relationships" (PDF). *Interpersonal Processes in Romantic Relationships. Handbook of Interpersonal Communication*. **3**: 643–679 – via Sage.

Jones, W.H., & Burdette, M.P. (1994). Betrayal in relationships. In A.L. Weber & J.H. Harvey (Eds.), *Perspectives on close relationships* (pp. 243–262). Boston: Allyn & Bacon.

Kingma, D.R. (1987). *Coming apart: Why relationships end and how to live through the ending of yours*. Berkeley, CA: Conari Press.

Leick, N., & Davidsen-Nielsen, M. (1991).

Healing pain: Attachment, loss, and grief therapy. (David Stoner, Tras.). New York: Tavistock/Routledge.

Neeld, E.H. (1990). *Seven choices: Taking the steps to a new life after losing someone you love.* New York: Dell Publishing.

Pennebaker, J. (1990). *Opening up: The healing power of confiding to others.* New York: Avon Books.

Phillips, D., & Judd, R. (1978). *How to fall out of love.* New York: Fawcett Popular Library.

Rollie, S. S. and S. W. Duck (2006). Stage theories of marital breakdown. Handbook of Divorce and Dissolution of Romantic Relationships. J. H. Harvey and M. A. Fine. Mahwah, NJ., Lawrence Erlbaum Associates: 176-193.

Zuckermann, Ghil'ad; et al. (2015), *Engaging – A Guide to Interacting Respectfully and Reciprocally with Aboriginal and Torres Strait Islander People, and their Arts Practices and Intellectual Property* (PDF), Australian Government: Indigenous Culture Support, p. 12, archived from the original (PDF) on 30 March 2016, retrieved 25 June 2016

The mathematical theory of communication. Urbana, Illinois: University of Illinois Press

Daniel Chandler, "The Transmission Model of

Communication", Aber.ac.ukArchived January 6, 2010, at the Wayback Machine

Stafford, L., & Merolla, A. (2007). Idealization, reunions, and stability in long distance dating relationships. Journal of Social and Personal Relationships, 37-54.

Johnson, A. (2001). Examining the maintenance of friendships: Are there differences between geographically close and long-distance friends? Communication Quarterly, 424-435.

Van Horn, K., Arnone, A., Nesbitt, K., Desilets, L., Sears, T., & Giffin, M. (1997). Physical distance and interpersonal characteristics in college students' romantic relationships. Personal Relationships, 15-24.

Mohr JJ, Daly CA (2008). "Sexual minority stress and changes in relationship quality in same-sex couples". *Journal of Social and Personal Relationships*. **25** (6): 989–1007. doi:10.1177/0265407508100311.

Li T, Dobinson C, Scheim A, Ross L (2013). "Unique Issues Bisexual People Face in Intimate Relationships: A Descriptive Exploration of Lived Experience". *Journal of Gay & Lesbian Mental Health*. **17**: 21–39. doi:10.1080/19359705.2012.723607.

Iantaffi A, Bockting WO (March 2011). "Views from both sides of the bridge? Gender, sexual legitimacy and transgender people's experiences of relationships". *Culture, Health & Sexuality*. **13** (3): 355–70. doi:10.1080/13691058.2010.537770. PMC 3076785. PMID 21229422.

DeHaan S, Kuper LE, Magee JC, Bigelow L, Mustanski BS (2013). "The interplay between online and offline explorations of identity, relationships, and sex: a mixed-methods study with LGBT youth". *Journal of Sex Research*. **50** (5): 421–34. doi:10.1080/00224499.2012.661489. PMID 22489658.

Roisman GI, Clausell E, Holland A, Fortuna K, Elieff C (January 2008). "Adult romantic relationships as contexts of human development: a multimethod comparison of same-sex couples with opposite-sex dating, engaged, and married dyads". *Developmental Psychology*. **44** (1): 91–101. doi:10.1037/0012-1649.44.1.91. PMID 18194008.

Number of U.S. adults cohabiting with a partner continues to rise, especially among those 50 and older". *Pew Research Center*. 2017-04-06. Retrieved 2018-04-04.

Dainton, M., & Aylor, B. (2001). A relational

uncertainty analysis of jealousy, trust, and maintenance in long-distance versus geographically close relationships. Communication Quarterly, 172-188.

Stafford, L., & Reske, J. (1990). Idealization and communication in long-distance premarital relationships. Family Relations, 274-279.

Knapp, M. L. (1978). Social intercourse: From greeting to goodbye (pp. 5-7). Boston: Allyn and Bacon.

Harper, Douglas. "communication". *Online Etymology Dictionary*. Retrieved 2013-06-23.

C.E. Shannon. "A Mathematical Theory of Communication" (PDF). *Math.harvard.edu*. Retrieved 2017-05-01.

"Types of Body Language". *Simplybodylanguage.com*. Retrieved 2016-02-08.

Wazlawick, Paul (1970's) opus

(Burgoon, J., Guerrero, L., Floyd, K., (2010). Nonverbal Communication, Taylor & Francis. p. 3)

Martin-Rubió, Xavier (2018-09-30). *Contextualising English as a Lingua Franca: From Data to Insights*. Cambridge Scholars Publishing. ISBN 978-1-5275-1696-0.

Ferguson, Sherry Devereaux; Lennox-Terrion, Jenepher; Ahmed, Rukhsana; Jaya, Peruvemba (2014). *Communication in Everyday Life: Personal and Professional Contexts*. Canada: Oxford University Press. p. 464. ISBN 9780195449280.

Xin Li. "Complexity Theory – the Holy Grail of 21st Century". Lane Dept of CSEE, West Virginia University. Archived from the original on 2013-08-15.

Bateson, Gregory (1960) Steps to an Ecology of Mind

communication". *The office of superintendent of Public Instruction*. Washington.